Although designing a symmetrical... rarely is. That's because it's hard to find two adjacent surfaces in a home that are actually level, plumb, and square. And, as soon as surfaces go out of square, you've got another layer of complexity in your pattern. That's why it's critical to check your surfaces before designing (see pages 54–55).

OUT-OF-SQUARE FLOOR. An out-of-square floor results in unattractive tapered tiles along one edge. The solution is to split the taper equally between the two sides.

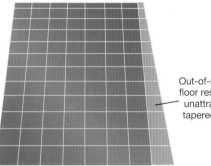

Out-of-square floor results in unattractive tapered tiles

OUT-OF-LEVEL FLOOR. An out-of-level floor is usually not noticeable unless tiles extend up the wall. There's not a lot you can do here except level the floor before tiling.

A floor that's not level isn't obvious unless the tile extends up the wall

TILE BASICS

To create a tile layout for a room, first make a preliminary drawing and define the tile/grout joint dimensions.

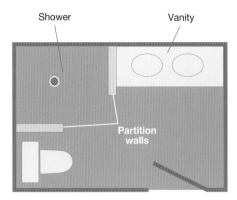

Shower   Vanity

Partition
walls

PRELIMINARY DRAWINGS. Your preliminary drawing doesn't need to be a work of art, but it does need to be to scale. One way to create a scale drawing is to use graph paper. If each square equals the size of your tiles, designing a pattern is greatly simplified. Measure a wall, and mark the corresponding length on the graph paper. Continue around the room and then add partition walls, doorways, and fixtures.

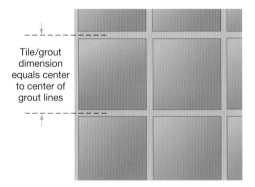

Tile/grout
dimension
equals center
to center of
grout lines

TILE/GROUT JOINT DIMENSIONS. To lay out tile precisely in a measured drawing, you need to know the dimensions for a full tile plus its grout line, as illustrated in the bottom drawing. See page 30 for recommended grout spacing for various sizes of tile.

Home How-To
Handbook
Tile

RICK PETERS

Sterling Publishing Co., Inc.
NEW YORK

Library of Congress Cataloging-in-Publication Data available
10 9 8 7 6 5 4 3 2 1

Published by Sterling Publishing Co., Inc.
387 Park Avenue South, New York, NY 10016

Distributed in Canada by Sterling Publishing
c/o Canadian Manda Group, 165 Dufferin Street,
Toronto, Ontario, Canada M6K 3H6
Distributed in the United Kingdom by GMC Distribution Services,
Castle Place, 166 High Street, Lewes, East Sussex, England BN7 1XU
Distributed in Australia by Capricorn Link (Australia) Pty. Ltd.
P.O. Box 704, Windsor, NSW 2756, Australia

Sterling ISBN-13: 978–1–4027–4810–3
          ISBN-10: 1–4027–4810–8

Book Design: Richard Oriolo
Photography: Christopher J. Vendetta
Page Layout: Sandy Freeman
Illustrations: Bob Crimi
Contributing Editor: Cheryl Romano
Copy Editor: Barbara McIntosh Webb
Indexer: Nan Badgett

For information about custom editions, special sales, premium and
corporate purchases, please contact Sterling Special Sales
Department at 800-805-5489 or specialsales@sterlingpub.com

Contents

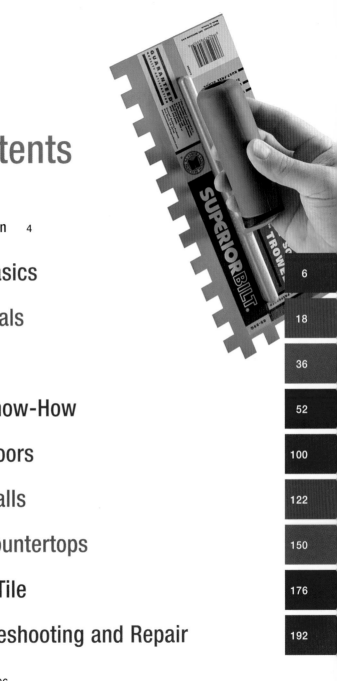

Introduction

FOR THE MODERN DO-IT-YOURSELFER, tile gives a world of options—and a tradition that stretches back thousands of years, to ancient Babylon. Yep, tile can be that durable, and even more versatile today. Let it make over floors, walls, countertops, outdoors or in, or just add an accent spark to almost anyplace in the home. From pastels to jewel tones, natural stone to glass, slick to patterned, tile today offers the colors, materials, patterns, and sizes to create anything you can imagine.

What's more, tile is actually easy to work with. Some types, especially ceramic tile, can be cut and shaped with a minimum of specialty tools. There's no denying that tiling is messier than many other home improvement processes, but it's worth the mess. Tile's durability lets it stand up to constant foot traffic, food spills, moisture— just about anything you can throw at it. It's easy to maintain and if installed properly will last for years and years.

How to Use This Book

There are roughly three sections: Basics, Projects, and Troubleshooting. The first section (chapters 1–4) starts with *Tile Basics,* where we explore common tile installations, as well as how to lay out and estimate tile. In *Materials* we guide you through the many types of tile, plus installation materials such as adhesives, grouts, and membranes. *Tools* details the specialty tools you'll need to work with tile. In *Tile Know-How,* you'll find the nuts and bolts of laying out, cutting, and installing tile. The second section, on Projects (chapters 5–8), includes *Tile Floors:* how to install just about every kind of tile flooring in your home. Then there's *Tile Walls,* including plain and patterned walls, plus a range mural. *Tile Countertops* covers standard countertops, along with backsplashes, kitchen islands, and bathroom sink tops. *Glass Tile* delves into the beautiful world of translucent tile. The final section is *Troubleshooting and Repair,* where we share a systematic approach to tracking down and solving common tile problems.

Codes and Permits

If any of your projects involve adding, extending, or modifying electrical or plumbing lines as well as framing, check with your local building inspector for permit and inspection requirements. Usually, an inspector will first check your work at the "rough-in" stage (no wall coverings in place) and again when all the finish work is done (fixtures installed). By making sure your work is done to code, an inspector helps protect both your family and your home.

1

Tile Basics

IF YOU LIKE TO DO IT YOURSELF, tile likes you, and it will remain friends for a long time: It's simple to install, stands up well, and just looks great. You can achieve a whole new look by using tile to make over a countertop, walls, and floors. Unlike sheet vinyl or carpeting, where the pattern is defined by the manufacturer, tiles are individual: They give you the freedom to create your own personalized designs. In this chapter, we'll cover the basics of designing with tile, how to estimate tile, and common methods of installation.

Tile Layout

When it comes to laying out tile, two rules are paramount: Be symmetrical, and hide the cut edges of partial tiles.

INCORRECT

CORRECT

BE SYMMETRICAL. When designing a layout for tile, position partial or cut tiles so they are equally balanced on a wall, floor, or countertop, as illustrated in the top drawing. When partial tiles are balanced, the eye tends to dismiss them. Without symmetry, the eye immediately notices the imbalance.

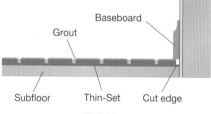

FLOOR

Baseboard

Grout

Subfloor   Thin-Set   Cut edge

HIDE CUT EDGES. The edges of most tiles are rounded to create a smooth transition for the grout that fills the gaps between the tiles. When you cut a tile, you create a sharp edge that is noticeably different from the rounded edges. As a general rule, these cut edges should always be hidden by some type of trim, as illustrated in the bottom drawing.

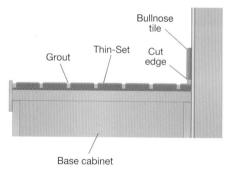

Bullnose tile

Thin-Set   Cut edge

Grout

Base cabinet

COUNTERTOP

Estimating Tile

There are two common ways to estimate how much tile you'll need for a job: square footage and individual tiles.

SQUARE FOOTAGE. Estimating tile via square footage is the more popular method because it's fast and easy. Simply multiply the length and width of the room and subtract any fixtures, etc., as illustrated in the top drawing. As a general rule you should add 20% to your calculation for miscuts and breakage.

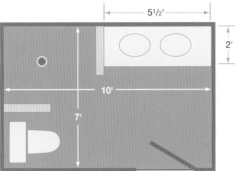

7' x 10'= 70 sq.ft., less the vanity's 11 sq.ft. = 59 sq.ft.

INDIVIDUAL TILES. Although estimating by counting tiles takes more time than square-footage estimation, it tends to be more accurate. To use this method you'll need to first mark the tile layout on your preliminary drawing, as illustrated in the bottom drawing. Then just count the tiles.

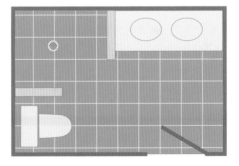

37 full tiles and 23 partial edge tiles and 12 partials = 60 tiles

37 tiles and 11 edge tiles and 12 partials = 60 tiles

Methods of Installation

To install tile, the most frequently used methods are thick-bed and thin-bed.

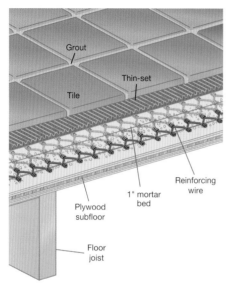

Grout

Thin-set

Tile

Reinforcing wire

1" mortar bed

Plywood subfloor

Floor joist

THICK-BED INSTALL. For years, all tile was set on a thick bed of mortar, as illustrated in the top drawing. But with the advent of modern backer boards (see below), this method became less popular. However, a thick-bed install is still the best choice when floors are highly uneven, and also in commercial areas: Thick-bed installations stand up better over time than thin-bed installs. The downside to a thick-bed install is that it takes considerable skill to lay a flat, thick bed of mortar.

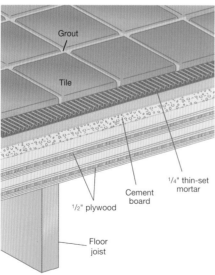

Grout

Tile

¹/₄" thin-set mortar

Cement board

¹/₂" plywood

Floor joist

THIN-BED INSTALL. All tile needs a flat, stable foundation. Modern backer board or cement board (page 32) provides this without the fuss of laying mortar. Sheets of cement board are fastened securely to the subfloor to create an excellent surface for tile, as shown in the bottom drawing.

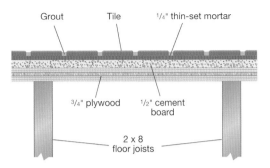

Grout   Tile   ¼" thin-set mortar

¾" plywood   ½" cement board

2 x 8 floor joists

TYPICAL TILED FLOOR. Most tile for floors is 12"×12" or larger and is bonded to ½"-thick cement board via a layer of thin-set mortar, as illustrated in the top drawing. At minimum, the subfloor should be at least ¾"-thick plywood. Two layers of ½" or ⅝" plywood are preferable.

TYPICAL TILED WALL. How tile is secured to a wall will depend on whether or not it will be subjected to moisture. In dry locations, the tile can be laid directly onto moisture-resistant drywall (page 33) or onto sheets of ¼" backer board attached to the drywall and studs. In either case, the tile is set into a layer of thin-set mortar, as illustrated in the bottom drawing. (For wet installs, see page 15.)

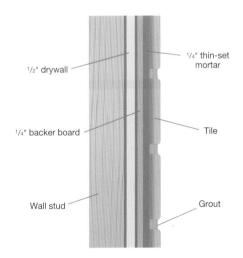

½" drywall   ¼" thin-set mortar

¼" backer board   Tile

Wall stud   Grout

TYPICAL TILED COUNTERTOP. When a countertop is tiled, the front and back edges need special attention. Usually, edging trim is used to make the transition from tile to cabinet at the front edge, and some type of trim creates a backsplash at the juncture of countertop and back wall, as illustrated in the top drawing.

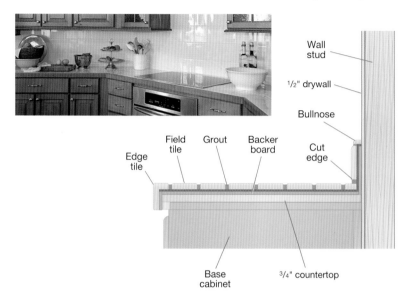

BACKSPLASH VARIATIONS. The bottom drawing illustrates three common methods to create a backsplash: bullnose, cove, and cap. The tile can attach directly to drywall, or to cement or backer board attached to the drywall and studs.

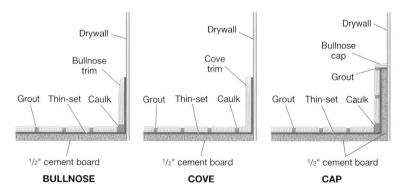

WET INSTALLS. You need to take extra precautions when installing tile in wet areas. This is because although most tile is impervious to water, the grout isn't (the exception to this is epoxy grout, which is fully waterproof). Even when you seal the porous grout (see page 31), moisture can still work its way past it. Then you can get weakening of the thin-set/tile bond, and even damage to the underlying drywall and framing.

To prevent this moisture damage, some type of waterproofing membrane must be installed between the tile and its backing, as illustrated in the bottom drawing. Waterproofing membranes are discussed on page 34, and their installation is covered on pages 80–82.

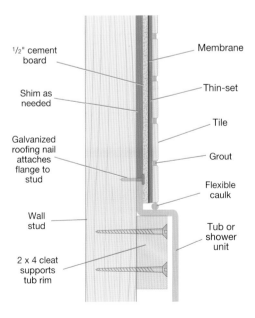

1/2" cement board

Shim as needed

Galvanized roofing nail attaches flange to stud

Wall stud

2 x 4 cleat supports tub rim

Membrane

Thin-set

Tile

Grout

Flexible caulk

Tub or shower unit

Expansion Joints

An expansion joint is a space or gap that allows adjoining materials to expand and contract without damaging each other. This gap is typically filled with a resilient material like silicone caulk. Expansion joints are necessary for floor perimeters, to break up large floors, and between countertops and their backsplashes.

FLOOR PERIMETERS. For floors that are less than 12 feet wide, the only expansion joints required are around the perimeter of the room, as illustrated in the drawing below.

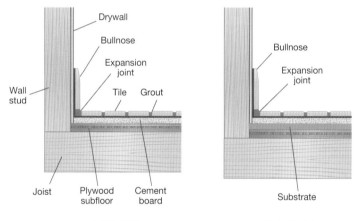

THIN-SET

THICK BED

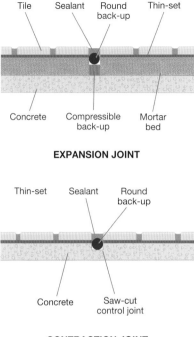

Tile   Sealant   Round   Thin-set
                   back-up

Concrete   Compressible   Mortar
            back-up   bed

EXPANSION JOINT

Thin-set   Sealant   Round
                       back-up

Concrete   Saw-cut
            control joint

CONTRACTION JOINT

LARGE FLOORS. For floors more than 12 feet wide, and when tile is installed over a concrete slab, you'll need expansion joints to keep the tile from damaging itself due to slab movement. On concrete slabs with expansion joints or control joints, you should position a tile expansion joint directly over the slab's joints, as illustrated in the top drawing.

COUNTERTOP AND COVE. Expansion joints are must-haves wherever there's a change in the backing material. The reason is simple: These materials will expand and contract at different rates and will cause problems if they're not separated by a flexible joint.

A common example of this is when a tiled countertop attached to cement or backer board meets a tiled drywall wall, as illustrated in the bottom drawing. Shown are three ways to create a flexible expansion joint that will allow movement without damage.

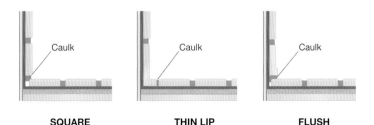

Caulk   Caulk   Caulk

SQUARE   **THIN LIP**   **FLUSH**

2

Materials

I N THE WORLD OF HOME IMPROVEMENT ELEMENTS, tile may be the ultimate multitasker: It works for floors, walls, countertops, and showers. With so many applications, tile not surprisingly offers lots of options, from type of material to size, color, pattern, and texture. But there's more to selecting the goods for a tile job than just picking out the tile. You'll also need to pick underlayment, adhesives, grout, and membranes. In this chapter, we'll guide you through these myriad options so you can choose what's best for your project.

Tile

When it's time to choose tile, it's important that you know about the properties of the different types, including ceramic, porcelain, glass, natural stone, terracotta, and quarry.

CERAMIC. By far the most common of all installed types of tile, ceramic tile is made by pressing clay into a shape, coating it with a glaze, and firing it to create a sturdy, colorful tile (top photo). Ceramic tile is inexpensive, easy to work with, and durable.

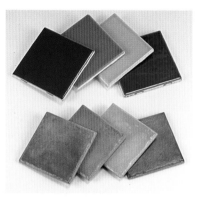

Ceramic Tile Ratings

The most-used system for rating ceramic tile is the Porcelain Enamel Institute (PEI) abrasion test; it's recommended by the American Society of Testing Materials (ASTM). These ratings measure the wear resistance of the tile surface. Tile grades are usually stamped on tile boxes and not on individual tiles.

CLASS	RATING	DESCRIPTION
1	No foot traffic	Ceramic tile suggested for interior residential and commercial wall applications only.
2	Light traffic	Ceramic tile suggested for interior residential and commercial wall applications and for residential bathroom floor applications only.
3	Light to moderate traffic	Ceramic tile suggested for residential floor, countertop, and wall applications.
4	Moderate to heavy traffic	Ceramic tile suggested for residential, medium commercial, and light institutional floor and wall applications.
5	Heavy to extra-heavy traffic	Ceramic tile suggested for residential, commercial, and institutional floor and wall applications subjected to heavy to extra-heavy traffic.

PORCELAIN. Porcelain tile (top left photo) looks a lot like standard ceramic tile, but it's made from refined white clay and is fired at much higher temperatures. The resulting tile is much less porous than ceramic tile, so it can stand up to freezing and thawing. This makes it ideal for outdoor applications. Porcelain tile tends to be more brittle than ceramic tile and is best cut with a motorized wet saw (page 41). Quality porcelain tile is frequently labeled on its back (top right).

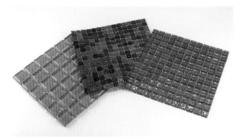

GLASS. Although glass tile has been around for a while, it has gained significant popularity only recently. Translucent and rich in color, glass is now one of the hottest tile materials around. Glass tile is impervious to moisture, so it's an excellent choice in bathrooms, especially as tub or shower surrounds. It's so hardy it can stand up to the outdoors and is often used for pool or spa linings.

Glass tile is cut with special tools (see pages 182–183) and should always be set in a white adhesive to prevent color distortion. The only downside to glass tile is that it's quite expensive—usually, 8 to 10 times the cost of ceramic tile.

NATURAL STONE.
Natural stone has been
a popular choice for
tiling since, naturally, it
provides a distinctive
appearance with richly
varying colors. Marble,
granite, and slate are the
most common. In terms
of hardness, granite is
the hardest, followed by
marble and slate. Marble
and slate stain easily

and should be sealed. Although beautiful, natural stone is expensive and tends to offer fewer trim choices than other tile materials.

TUMBLED STONE. A popular version of natural stone is tumbled stone (bottom photo). Any of the natural stones can be tumbled in abrasives and bathed in acid to create rounded edges and a rough, rustic appearance. Marble and slate are the most common stones tumbled; each piece is unique and offers a rough-hewn look that you won't find elsewhere. Because of the added tumbling process, tumbled stone is quite expensive. If money is tight, consider using it only as an accent.

TERRA-COTTA. Terra-cotta means "cooked earth" and has been around for centuries. It is made from unrefined clay baked at low temperatures. In days past, the sun supplied the heat. Nowadays, terra-cotta is fired in a kiln. But unlike on ceramic tiles, no glaze is used

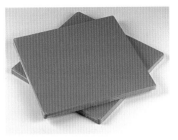

(top photo). This means that the tile needs sealing once it has been installed, to prevent staining. Terra-cotta tile is inexpensive but offers few color and trim choices.

QUARRY. Quarry tile used to come from a quarry, of course. But today, quarry tile is fashioned from red clay to resemble the quarried tile of yesteryear (middle photo). Quarry tile is typically dark in color, with a rough surface and striated back to help with mortar adhesion.

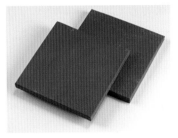

Like terra-cotta tile, quarry tile is unglazed and must be sealed after installation to prevent staining. Also like terra-cotta tile, quarry tile is inexpensive, but offers limited color choice and few trim options.

Tile Comparison

MATERIAL	ADVANTAGES	DISADVANTAGES	COST
Ceramic	Easy to work with; huge variety	Not freeze/thaw stable	$
Porcelain	Freeze/thaw stable	Difficult to cut, tends to be brittle	$$
Marble	Natural variations in color provide great depth	Porous, stains, needs periodic sealing	$$$
Terra-cotta	Highly variable surface is quite rustic and is slip-resistant	Few color choices (yellow to brown to red), must be sealed	$
Quarry	Rough-hewn surface is attractive and slip-resistant	Open texture requires periodic maintenance	$
Glass	Translucent; impervious to moisture	Can scratch, must be installed with white adhesive	$$$$

Tile Size, Shape, and Texture

Regardless of the material it's made of, all tile comes in one of two forms: loose tile or sheet-mounted (top photo).

LOOSE TILES. Loose tiles come in wide variety of shapes and sizes, as illustrated in the bottom drawing. Sizes range from 1"×1" to 12"×12" squares. Flooring tile frequently comes in larger format, including 14"×14" and 16"×16". Loose tiles smaller than 2" square are usually mounted on sheets (see the opposite page). Shapes vary from squares and rectangles to octagons and ogees. It's important to note that 4"×4" tile is rarely 4" square. Size and consistency vary widely from manufacturer to manufacturer and often even within tile from a single manufacturer. That's why you should always have your tile on hand when designing a layout; see page 10.

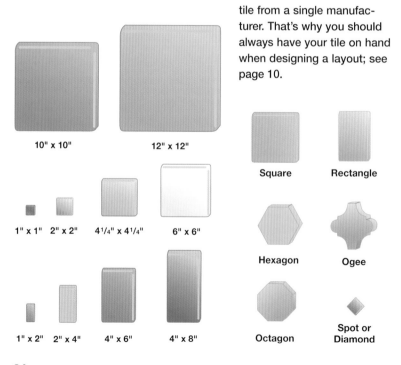

10" x 10"　　12" x 12"

1" x 1"　2" x 2"　4¹/₄" x 4¹/₄"　6" x 6"

1" x 2"　2" x 4"　4" x 6"　4" x 8"

Square　Rectangle

Hexagon　Ogee

Octagon

Spot or Diamond

SHEET-MOUNTED TILE.
Sheet-mounted tile is often called mosaic tile (top photo). Mosaic tile is any tile that's less than 2" square. Small tiles like this are frequently mounted on sheets to make installation faster. The sheet backing can be paper, plastic mesh, or a grid of rubber dots. The most common sheet size is 12" square, but many other sizes are available, depending on the tile design. Sheet-mounted tiles come in a variety of patterns, ranging from a simple stacked pattern to more complex herringbone and octagon patterns, as illustrated in the drawing at right.

Staggered or Running Bond

Stacked

Herringbone

Herringbone Wrap

Decorative Octagon

Decorative Stagger

MATERIALS

TEXTURES. Another thing to look for when selecting tile is texture. Texture varies from flat and glossy to highly textured 3D, like the tiles shown in the bottom photo. Texture can add a whole other dimension to a tiled project. Just keep in mind that smooth, flat tile is much easier to clean and maintain compared to highly textured tile. Texture is very important when selecting floor tile. All floor tile should be textured and not smooth, to prevent slipping.

Specialty Tiles

In addition to standard tiles (frequently called field tiles, since these cover the bulk of the tiled area, or field), there are lots of specialty tiles. Decorative tiles, liners, and listellos add a distinctive touch to a tile job, and trim tiles serve as transitions from one surface to another.

DECORATIVE TILES. Decorative tiles are a great way to add an accent to an otherwise ordinary tile project. Decorative tiles can be whimsical or formal, classic or modern. Some are mass-produced, others are hand-painted. Sizes, textures, and colors vary greatly, as shown in the top left photo. You'll also find sheet-mounted decorative tiles in all sorts of designs (top right photo).

LINERS. Liners are narrow tiles that are used to make borders and lines in tile designs, as shown in the bottom photo. Liners can be loose or sheet-mounted, as pictured. We used sheet-mounted liners for the tiled tub surround shown on page 139 and for the range mural shown on page 148.

LISTELLOS. Roughly translated from Italian, listello means "border". But what differentiates a listello from a liner is texture. Liners are flat, while listellos offer shape and texture, as shown in the top photo. Common shapes

include chair rail, pencils, rope, and beads. Just as with liners, listellos are a great way to add an accent, highlight an area, or break up a wide expanse of tile. An example of installed listellos is shown on page 128.

TRIM. Trim tile serves as a transition from one surface to another. Common trim tiles are shown in the bottom drawing and include bullnose, cove, and counter edging. Bullnose can be used as cove base for tile flooring, as a backsplash for a counter, or as a transition from tile to another surface, such as tiled tub surround to the adjacent drywall. Cove can also be used as cove base for flooring and as a back-splash for a counter.

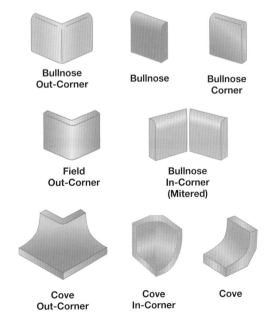

Bullnose
Out-Corner

Bullnose

Bullnose
Corner

Field
Out-Corner

Bullnose
In-Corner
(Mitered)

Cove
Out-Corner

Cove
In-Corner

Cove

Adhesives

There are two basic types of adhesive used to bond tile to a surface: thin-set mortar and organic mastics.

THIN-SET MORTAR. Thin-set mortar typically comes in dry form and needs to be mixed on site with either water or an additive mix (top and middle photos). Some thin-set mortars called polymer-modified thin-sets have additives included in the dry mix so that all it takes is water at the site. As a general rule, thin-set mortars have much greater bonding and compression strength than organic mastics. They are also more flexible and tend to set up faster. Because of their greater compression strength, thin-set mortars are usually specified for floor installations. Additives or add-mixes can be mixed with the dry powder to create mortar that has greater bond and compression strength compared to standard thin-set. Plus, they offer even better flexibility.

QUICK FIX

Ready-Made Thin-Set

When you're in a hurry or just don't feel like dealing with the mess of mixing up a batch of thin-set, consider using one of the new ready-made thin-set products that are now available. Although these mixes tend to have a fairly strong chemical smell, they certainly are convenient. Just pry off the lid and you're ready to go.

EPOXY-BASED THIN-SET. Epoxy-based thin-sets are a specialty thin-set made up of three parts: a liquid resin, a liquid hardener, and a powdered filler. Epoxy thin-sets are much more expensive than standard thin-sets but have a couple of advantages over them. First, an epoxy thin-set can adhere tile to just about any surface, including metal. Second, although the thin-set isn't waterproof, it is highly water-resistant. With the proper membrane (see page 34), epoxy thin-sets can be used in both wet and dry applications.

ORGANIC MASTICS. You can't buy them in a health-food store, but you can buy organic mastics with either a latex or petroleum base. They are made up of two parts: a bonding agent and a carrier. With a petroleum-based mastic, the carrier is solvent; with latex, it's water. Organic mastics are inexpensive, ready to use, and easy to work with. Because they lack the bond and compression strength of thin-set, organic mastics are usually used only to adhere wall tile to drywall or plywood. And because they are less flexible than thin-set, the underlying foundation must be perfectly flat to achieve a good bond.

Properties of Adhesives

TYPE OF ADHESIVE	ADVANTAGES	DISADVANTAGES
Thin-set	Great bond and compression strength. Sets up quick. Very flexible. Recommended for floors.	Must be mixed on site. Can set up too quickly. Tools, spills need to be cleaned immediately.
Organic mastic	No prep or mixing. Easier to use than thin-sets. Great adhesion makes them perfect for wall tile.	Inferior bond and compression strength when compared to thin-set. Not as flexible as thin-set.

Grout

Contrary to popular belief, grout does not hold tile in place—the adhesive does that. Grout's job is to fill the gap between the tiles to both support the edges of

tile and frame the tile. Grout usually comes in a dry powder and can be mixed on site with water or an add-mix to increase bond strength and flexibility. Grout comes in many colors but only two basic types: unsanded and sanded, as shown in the top photo.

UNSANDED GROUT. Unsanded or non-sanded grout is basically cement mixed with additives and color. An additive improves spreadability and retards the curing time to give you more time to work with. Unsanded grout should be used to fill only gaps that are less than $1/16$" wide. For gaps larger than that, go with sanded grout.

SANDED GROUT. With sanded grout, sand is added to the mix for increased strength. Sanded grout is used to fill gaps between tiles that are greater than $1/16$". Both sanded and unsanded grout are forced into the gaps between tiles with a special tool called a grout float (see page 49). The amount of grout you'll need for a project will depend on the size of the tiles and the width of the gap or grout joint, as shown in the table below.

Grout Coverage versus Tile Size

SIZE OF TILE	WIDTH OF JOINT*			
	1/8"	1/4"	3/8"	1/2"
1" × 1"	30			
2" × 2"	16	52		
4" × 5"	15	30	45	60
6" × 6"	25	50	75	100
8" × 8"	12.5	25	37.5	50

*The numbers in the width-of-joint section describe how many pounds of dry grout are needed to cover 100 square feet of tile.

STAIN-PROOF GROUT. Even when properly applied, both sanded grout and unsanded grout are very porous and stain easily. That's why it's important for you to seal the grout (see the sidebar below). An alternative developed by TrafficMaster in conjunction with 3M is stain-proof grout (top photo). TrafficMaster Stainproof Grout™ is premixed and resistant to common household stains like wine, coffee, ketchup, shoe polish, etc. TrafficMaster Stainproof Grout™ with Scotchgard Protector carries a 25-year Performance Warranty, which guarantees that the product will resist household stains, as well as mold, mildew, and color fading.

PRO TIP

Grout Sealers

◤◣ Most sanded and unsanded grout is quite porous once it has dried. So it's important to seal the grout to prevent moisture from seeping through the grout and causing damage. Sealing the grout will also help prevent staining. Grout sealers typically come in a bottle with a built-in applicator, like the one shown in the photo at right. The number one mistake most people make with a grout sealer is not waiting the recommended time for the grout to completely dry—usually a minimum of 48 hours (more in humid areas). Sealing damp grout just seals in moisture, leading to mold and mildew.

Underlayment

Tile can be successfully adhered to a variety of underlying surfaces, including backer board, concrete, plywood, and moisture-resistant drywall.

BACKER BOARD. Backer board, called CBU's in the trade (cementitious backer units), is fast becoming the most common underlayment for tile. Backer board comes in two basic types: a core of sand and cement that's covered with a layer of reinforcing mesh (bottom board in top photo), and a mixture of sand, cement, and mineral fibers (top board in top photo). These are sold under the brand names WonderBoard and HardieBacker, respectively. WonderBoard comes in ¼" and ½" thicknesses and has dots screened onto one side at 6" intervals as a guide for fastener placement. The sheets are 3'×5' and 3'×8'. HardieBacker comes in three sizes: 3'×5', 4'×4', and 4'×8', in both ¼" and ½" thicknesses. The surface is dotted for fastener placement, and a grid is stamped onto one face as a cutting guide. Both are attached with screws or galvanized nails. For more on working with and installing backer board, see pages 72–77.

CONCRETE SLAB. A concrete slab (bottom photo) is an excellent foundation for tile, as long as it's level, sound, and dry. See page 68 for more on determining whether your concrete is suitable for tile.

PLYWOOD. Before CBU's, tile floors were often installed on plywood. Because wood moves with changes in humidity, many of these floors ended up with failed adhesive/tile bonds. If you must tile directly onto plywood, make sure it's rated for exterior use and is defect-free. If it isn't, consider adding a thin layer of exterior-rated plywood on top of the existing subfloor.

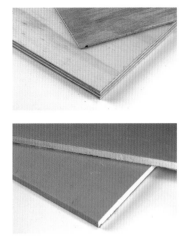

MOISTURE-RESISTANT DRY-WALL. Moisture-resistant drywall (commonly referred to as greenboard) is a suitable underlayment for wall tile in a dry area. If used in a wet area, it must first be covered with a waterproofing membrane as described on page 34.

QUICK FIX

Self-Leveling Compounds

Floors are often uneven. To fix this, they need to be leveled by floating a layer of mortar on the floor— and this takes considerable skill. Fortunately, adhesive manufacturers have come up with a no-skill-needed option: self-leveling compounds. Self-leveling compounds come in a powdered form and can be mixed with water or an additive.

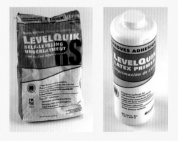

Once mixed, you simply pour the compound onto the floor and it will find its own level—what could be easier? The only downside is that they're quite expensive compared to mortar or cement mix.

Membranes

There are two types of membranes that you may need to install between your tile and underlayment: isolation and waterproofing membranes.

Isolation membranes

Isolation membranes are inserted between tile and an underlayment to prevent any movement in the underlayment from damaging the tile. They are usually made from cork or other flexible material to provide both isolation and some cushioning.

Waterproofing membranes

When you need to tile a wet area, you'll want to add a membrane between the tile and the underlayment to prevent moisture from seeping through and causing damage.

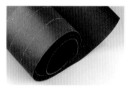

TAR PAPER. Tar paper is inexpensive, is readily available, and can be fastened directly to studs or drywall with staples.

SHEET MEMBRANES. Plastic sheathing is an inexpensive alternative to tar paper; just make sure it's at least 4 mils thick. Other sheet membranes include chlorinated polyethylene sandwiched between layers of woven polyester, and a pan liner (used to line the pan of tiled showers).

TROWEL-ON MEMBRANES. Trowel-on membranes are great for small, complex places where working with a sheet membrane would be difficult. All are designed to be used with some type of reinforcing material like fiberglass or woven polyester.

Expansion Joints

Wood is hygroscopic—that is, it constantly expands and contracts as the moisture in the air (humidity) changes. Odds are that the underlying structure and foundation of your home is made of wood. This means that your home is constantly moving. So whenever you attach a material that's non-hygroscopic (like tile) to a hygroscopic material (like a plywood subfloor), you need to create gaps—expansion joints—between the materials for movement. Expansion joints are typically filled with a flexible material like caulk or fiberglass tape.

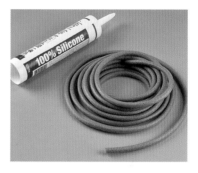

CAULK. Silicone caulk is the number one material used to fill expansion joints that are visible. For large joints, foam rod (commonly called caulk saver) is first inserted in the joint and then caulk is applied. Make sure to always use 100% silicone caulk for maximum flexibility.

FIBERGLASS TAPE. Backer boards are frequently installed with expansion joints between the sheets. To present an unbroken surface to the tile, these joints are covered with fiberglass tape and a coat of thin-set (for more on using fiberglass tape, see page 136).

3

Tools

THE TOOLS YOU'LL NEED to work with tile can be broadly grouped into four categories: measuring and marking, cutting, setting, and grouting. In this chapter, you'll learn the difference between a notched trowel and a margin trowel, and a tile nipper and a snap cutter. We'll also cover the special tools used for tile repair, as well as the gear you'll need to work safely.

Measuring and Marking

Laying out the tile is the foundation for every successful tile project. The measuring and marking tools you'll need to get an accurate layout include: levels, framing and combination squares, tape measures, chalk lines, contour gauges, compasses, and sliding bevels.

LEVELS. The most common levels are 3' or 4' long, with bodies made of wood, metal, or plastic; smaller torpedo levels are useful in tight spots. Virtually every level has multiple vials, which are curved glass or plastic tubes filled with alcohol (hence the name "spirit" level). A bubble of air trapped in the vial will always float to the highest point on the curve.

FRAMING SQUARE. A framing square is useful for checking walls, floors, and ceilings for square, as well as laying out complex patterns. We prefer an aluminum square to a steel one since it's much lighter and won't rust over time.

COMBINATION SQUARE. A combination square is a metal rule with a groove in it that accepts a pin in the head of the square. The head has two faces—one at 90 degrees, the other at 45 degrees. When the knurled nut on the end of the pin is tightened, the head locks the rule in place at the desired location.

TAPE MEASURE. When you're buying a tape measure, skip the bargain bin; it pays to buy quality. Go with a name brand you can trust. And take the time to check the tape for accuracy at the store. To do this, simply extend the tape out several feet and bend it back on itself. Align the inch marks and check to see if the graduations are even. On cheaper tapes, you'll often find that the graduations don't match up.

CHALK LINE. Chalk lines are useful for marking long, straight lines. Make sure to shake the chalk line before use to evenly coat the line. Hook one end at your mark, stretch the line to the opposite end, and pull the line straight up a couple of inches; then let go to "snap" a line.

PRO TIP

Laser Levels

Some tiling jobs, like tiling a wall with a chair rail, require drawing a line around the perimeter of a room. You could snap a chalk line, but then you'd be faced with finding a way to remove blue chalk from your walls. A better method is to use a laser level like the one shown in the photo below. Laser levels are coming down in cost, and can also be rented at most home and rental centers. The big advantage of a laser level is that it shoots a perfectly level line along a wall—or around the perimeter of a room— without leaving any marks.

TOOLS

CONTOUR GAUGE. A contour gauge lets you accurately copy the irregular shape of an obstacle such as a pipe or door casing and then transfer it onto your tile. To use the gauge, hold it flat and press it into the object. The many, moveable "fingers" of the gauge will conform to the object and retain its shape. Now you can pull it away and copy the shape onto the tile with a pencil or marking pen.

COMPASS. A compass is useful for laying out circles and arcs. The most common type is the wing compass, which has legs hinged at the top. One leg has a steel point and the other holds a standard pencil.

SLIDING BEVEL. A sliding bevel is invaluable for verifying angles, setting tools to match angles, and laying out virtually any angle. Most sliding bevels feature a metal slotted blade and a stock or body made of wood, plastic, or metal, available in a variety of sizes. The blade conveniently slips into the slot in the body for storage. The blade is locked in place by tightening a thumbscrew, wing nut, lever, or knob at the base of the stock.

Tile-Cutting Tools

The tools you'll need to cut tile will depend mostly on what material you're cutting. Ceramic tile cuts easily with snap cutters, rod saws, and tile nippers. Tougher materials like porcelain and glass are best cut with a motorized wet saw or with power tools fitted with abrasive blades (see page 44).

SNAP CUTTER. A snap cutter is basically a glass cutter fitted onto a sliding track designed for straight cuts. You score the surface of a tile by dragging the cutting wheel over the surface. Then you snap the tile at the scored line by pressing down on the wings on the front of the handle.

MOTORIZED WET SAW. A motorized wet saw fitted with a diamond blade will plow through almost any tile material. Either water is pumped onto the blade or the blade is immersed in water to both keep the blade cool and help wash away tile dust and debris.

ROTARY GRINDER. A rotary grinder when fitted with an abrasive blade is handy for making partial cuts in tile. Just be sure to securely clamp the tile to a work surface before making a cut.

HANDHELD TILE CUTTER. A handheld tile cutter is a portable version of the snap cutter. It combines a cutting wheel and snapping wings in one compact tool. Its only disadvantage is that you must use a straightedge to guide the cutting wheel when scoring a tile.

TILE NIPPER. A tile nipper, or "biter" as it's often referred to in the trade, is the number one tool for making curved cuts. The sharp jaws, when closed around a tile, will break or bite off a small portion of the tile. Nippers are frequently used in conjunction with a tile saw to make partial and curved cuts (for more on using tile nippers, see page 94). Glass tiles require their own special nipper (see page 183).

ELECTRIC DRILL AND MASONRY BITS. When it comes time to tile around pipes, you'll often need to drill holes in tile. Additionally, if you need to mount a fixture to a tiled floor or wall, you'll first need to drill access holes in the tile for the fasteners. An electric drill fitted with standard masonry bits will handle most jobs. But for larger holes and smoother cuts, you'll want to use a specialty bit; see the sidebar below.

PRO TIP

Drilling in Tile

There are two types of specialty bits that you'll find work better in tile than masonry bits. While masonry bits tend to leave rough and chipped holes and come in limited sizes, glass and tile bits are designed to make smooth cuts, and diamond hole saws handle large holes with ease. For more on drilling tile, see page 95.

TOOLS

GLASS AND TILE BITS. Technically, glass and tile bits with their pointed tips don't drill holes. Instead of a cutting action, they grind away material to leave a super-smooth hole.

DIAMOND HOLE SAWS. The cutting edge of a diamond hole saw is impregnated with diamond dust. This allows it to grind right through most tile, leaving a perfectly round hole.

ROD SAW. A rod saw is similar to a hacksaw in that the cutting blade (in this case an abrasive rod) is held in a handled frame. The throat of the frame is typically wider than a hacksaw to enable deeper cuts into a tile. Note that instead of cutting or slicing, you're grinding away tile material here, so it's pretty slow going. For quicker cuts, see the sidebar below.

PRO TIP

Tile-Cutting Blades for Power Tools

Manufacturers of power tool accessories produce a variety of abrasive cutting blades for portable power tools such as saber saws and reciprocating saws. In most cases, a standard high-speed steel (HSS) blade is coated with carbide particles or diamond dust. Here again, the action this produces is grinding versus cutting or slicing. But because the tool supplies the elbow grease, cuts can be made faster and with much less effort.

MASONRY RUBBING STONE. Whenever you cut a tile, you create a sharp edge. A masonry rubbing stone is a block of abrasive that you can use to smooth and even round over edges as needed. In many cases, the cutting action of the stone can be enhanced with a little water. Some stones are two stones in one— two thin layers of different grits are bonded together to provide either aggressive or fine cutting action.

CHISELS WITH SAFETY GRIPS

To replace a cracked or broken tile, one of the first things you need to do is remove the damaged tile. This usually entails breaking up the tile into smaller chunks and then chiseling these out. It's important to note that when you break and chisel tile, many small, needle-like frag-ments often frac-ture and shoot off in all directions. Eye protection is essential here. Another way you can protect both your eyes and your hands is to use a chisel with a safety grip like the one shown here. The rubber guard on the end not only protects your hand from an errant hammer strike, but it also helps deflect broken fragments flying toward your face.

Tile-Setting Tools

T he tools needed to set tile include trowels for applying adhesive, mixing paddles for mixing thin-set, tile spacers, and a mallet to level the tiles.

NOTCHED TROWEL. The notched trowel is the primary tool for applying adhesive. The notches may be V-shaped, U-shaped, or square. Various sizes and spacing handle various tile types and sizes (see the drawing below for recommended sizing). A notched trowel produces a ridged bed of adhesive that the tile is positioned on; when the tile is pressed down, the adhesive spreads out into the gaps to create a uniform bond.

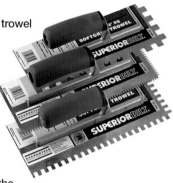

$3/16$ x $5/32$ **V**

$3/16$" $5/32$"

Adhesives;
Wall tile 6" or smaller

$3/16$ x $1/4$ **V**

$3/16$" $1/4$"

Adhesives;
Wall tile 6" or 12"

$5/16$ x $1/4$ x $1/16$ **V**

$1/16$" $5/16$" $1/4$"

Adhesives;
Wall tile 8" or 16"

$1/4$ x $5/16$ x $1/4$ **U**

$1/4$" $1/4$" $5/16$"

Thin-set;
Tile 8" or smaller

$1/4$ x $3/8$ x $1/4$ **U**

$1/4$" $3/8$"

Thin-set;
Tile 8" to 12"

$1/4$ x $1/2$ x $1/4$ **U**

$1/4$" $1/4$" $1/2$"

Thin-set;
Tile 12" or larger

$3/4$ x $9/16$ x $3/8$ **U**

$3/8$" $3/4$" $9/16$"

Medium bed or marble and granite mortars; marble, granite, or natural stone

$1/4$ x $1/4$ x $1/4$ **SQ**

$1/4$" $1/4$" $1/4$"

Thin-set;
Tile 8" or smaller

$1/4$ x $3/8$ x $1/4$ **SQ**

$1/4$" $1/4$" $3/8$"

Thin-set;
Tile 8" to 16"

$1/2$ x $1/2$ x $1/2$ **SQ**

$1/2$" $1/2$" $1/2$"

Thin-set or medium bed mortar;
Tile 16" or larger, pavers, and natural stone

MARGIN AND EDGING TROWELS.
Margin and edging trowels are the
long, thin cousins of notched
trowels and straight trowels.
They're used in places that
the larger tools can't
access. As with stan-
dard trowels,
they come in
a variety of
notch pat-
terns and sizes.

POINTER. A pointer is a special
trowel that has a pointed tip to let you
get into tight corners where a standard or
margin trowel can't. Pros often use these
to back-butter tiles (see page 85 for
more on back-buttering).

MIXING PADDLE. Powdered grout
and thin-set are mixed with water or
add-mix to create an easily spreadable
product. A mixing paddle
like the one shown here
will do this job in a jiffy.
Because of the torque
required to mix grout and
thin-set, make sure to use a
heavy-duty corded drill—stay
away from cordless drills for this
task, as it's easy to overheat them.

TILE SPACERS. In order to create uniform grout lines, the gaps between tiles must be consistent. The most accurate way to do this is to use rubber tile spacers. These cross-shaped spacers come in standard grout widths, including $\frac{1}{16}$", $\frac{1}{8}$", $\frac{3}{16}$", $\frac{1}{4}$", and $\frac{3}{8}$". For more on using tile spacers, see page 88.

DENTAL PICK. Tile spacers are designed to be placed between tiles vertically, not horizontally. If they're placed horizontally, it can be extremely difficult to remove them before grout is applied. A dental pick like the one shown here is an excellent tool for removing flat spacers (see page 89).

HAMMER AND RUBBER MALLET. You'll likely need both a hammer and a rubber mallet for your tile installation. The hammer is used for attaching cleats and battens to support tile, and the rubber mallet is used to set tile— typically with the aid of a shop-made caul; see page 89.

Grout Tools

The tools for applying grout are few and simple: a grout float, a grout bag, and a bucket and sponge.

GROUT FLOAT. A grout float presses grout into the gaps between tiles. Most sport a firm rubber base covered with a slick layer of plastic. These attach to a wood, metal, or plastic carrier with a handle. The float is held flat to press in grout and tilted at 45 degrees to squeegee off excess grout. For more on using a grout float, see page 96–98.

GROUT BAG. A grout bag is handy for grouting large tiles where the gaps between tiles are widely spaced apart. Instead of floating grout over the entire face of the tile and pressing it into joints, a grout bag works just like the icing bag that a pastry chef uses to decorate a cake. Just fill the bag with grout and twist and compress it to squeeze grout out of its tip, directly into the gaps in the tiles. This lets you apply grout with minimal mess.

SPONGE, BUCKET, AND CLOTH. After grout has been pressed into the gaps between tiles and the excess has been squeegeed off, remove residue with a damp sponge. Then allow the grout to dry to a haze, which is removed by buffing with a clean cloth.

Grout-Removal Tools

Over time, grout will deteriorate and fail. When this happens, you'll need to re-grout. To do this, you'll first need to remove the existing grout with either a grout saw, a rotary tool, or a grout-removal attachment; see below.

GROUT SAW. The blade on a grout saw is usually covered with carbide or tungsten bits and offset as shown to make it easier to use. Grout saws work great but require a lot of energy to use—especially if you're removing a lot of grout.

ROTARY TOOL. A rotary tool fitted with a grinding or grout-removal bit can supply the much-needed elbow grease for removing a lot of grout.

GROUT-REMOVAL ATTACH-MENT. Dremel makes a nifty attachment for their rotary tool (www.dremel.com) that does a terrific job of removing grout from ceramic tile with built-in spacers. The unique shape of the attachment keeps the grinding bit at the perfect cutting angle, and also keeps the cutting bit centered between the tiles. For more on using this attachment, see page 202.

Safety Gear

With any home improvement project it's important to don appropriate safety gear. For tiling, this includes eye, ear, and lung protection, gloves, and knee pads.

SAFETY GLASSES, EAR PROTECTORS, AND RESPIRATOR. Whenever you cut or break tile, you should always wear safety glasses. Tiny, sharp fragments of tile—particularly glazed and glass tile—can and will fracture and fly off in  all directions. The last place you want these is in your eyes. If you're using any power tools, including a motorized wet saw, protect your ears from the high-pitched whine of universal motors. Hearing loss can result from extended exposure to these high frequencies. Also, when you mix powdered grout and thin-set, protect your lungs from dangerous chemicals by wearing a respirator.

GLOVES AND KNEE PADS. Cut tile is sharp, so protect your hands with a pair of good-quality leather gloves. You should also know that many mastics and mortars can irritate skin, so  wear rubber gloves, as described on page 86. Finally, although not technically safety gear, a good set of knee pads will protect and cushion your knees from hard surfaces.

4

Tile Know-How

WHILE TILE VARIES WIDELY in colors, shapes, and materials, installing it takes skills that are pretty much standard. You'll need to know how to check surfaces for plumb, square, and level, how to lay out a project, how to prepare surfaces (including installing an underlayment or membrane), how to mix and apply adhesives and grout, and finally how to cut tile. We'll explore all these basics in this chapter.

Checking for Plumb, Square, and Level

In order to tile an area, you should know what challenges await. Are the floors level and the walls plumb? Are adjacent surfaces square? Is the area you'll be tiling square? Any deviation from level, plumb, and square will affect your project.

CHECKING A FLOOR FOR LEVEL. As long as you aren't extending floor tile up a wall, the eye can rarely see a floor that's out of level. So why bother checking it? Because an uneven floor will not support tile uniformly. Dips and lows, if not leveled, create potential areas for damage. Since an unlevel tile ends up unsupported, breakage is imminent. That's why you should check the floor with a level or a straightedge, mark any lows or highs, and correct these before tiling (see page 33 for self-levelers).

CHECKING A WALL FOR PLUMB. When you tile a wall that's out of plumb, you'll end up with tapered tiles on one or both sides. It's important to know about this in advance so that you can shift the tile from side to side as needed (see page 59 for more on this). Make sure to check the wall at both ends and at various points in between.

CHECKING ADJACENT SURFACES FOR SQUARE. Adjacent surfaces that are to be tiled but aren't square to each other—like the tub surround shown here—can cause problems with your tile patterns. What works on one end of the surround may not work on the other. That's why you should check and note any discrepancies and check your pattern with a story stick, as described on page 131.

as described on page 131.

P R O T I P

3-4-5 Triangle

A reliable way to check whether reference lines are exactly perpendicular is to use a 3-4-5 triangle. Start by measuring and marking a point 3 feet from the center-point where the lines cross (make this mark on either line), as shown. Then measure 4 feet from the centerpoint on the adjacent line and make a mark. Now measure from the 3-foot mark to the 4-foot mark. The lines are perpendicular if it measures exactly 5 feet. If it isn't, the lines aren't perpendicular and one of the lines will have to be adjusted.

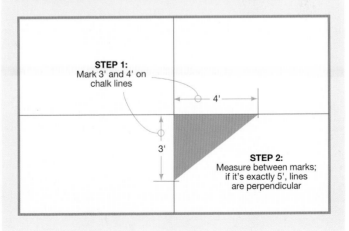

STEP 1:
Mark 3' and 4' on chalk lines

4'

3'

STEP 2:
Measure between marks; if it's exactly 5', lines are perpendicular

TILE KNOW-HOW

Laying Out a Floor

Laying out a tile pattern on floors can be tricky. In addition to complex shapes (page 57) and doorways, what makes floors difficult to lay out is that adjacent walls are rarely square, and opposite walls are often not parallel.

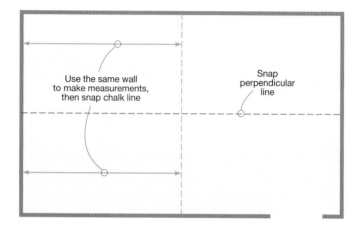

Use the same wall to make measurements, then snap chalk line

Snap perpendicular line

LOCATE CENTERLINES AND SNAP. To lay out a floor, you'll want to locate and snap centered reference lines. To get around the problem of unparallel walls, it's best to do this by first measuring out from the same wall to create your first line, as illustrated in the drawing above. Then use a framing square (page 38)—or better yet, a 3-4-5 triangle (page 55)—to locate and snap a centered line perpendicular to your first line, as shown. Once you've located and snapped your centerlines, you should test your tile pattern on the floor (page 116) and adjust the reference lines as needed to create even, partial tiles (if applicable) at the walls (see page 8).

LAYING OUT COMPLEX FLOORS. The secret to laying out a complex floor is to break it up into smaller, less complicated areas. Then you can treat each area independently. What's important, though, is to locate and snap one main reference line that you can use to create smaller patterns within the room, as illustrated in the drawing below. Note how the laundry room is treated separately from the kitchen area. Also note how the tile pattern was shifted to allow for full tiles at the transition between the tiled kitchen floor and the carpeted dining room.

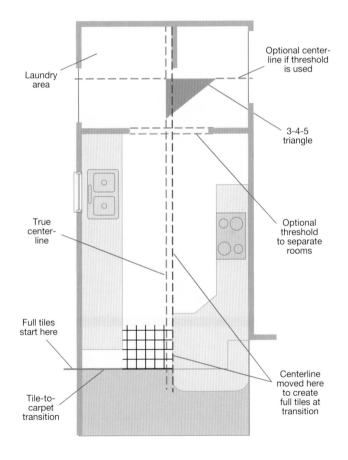

Laundry area

Optional center-line if threshold is used

3-4-5 triangle

True center-line

Optional threshold to separate rooms

Full tiles start here

Tile-to-carpet transition

Centerline moved here to create full tiles at transition

Making Minor Adjustments

So you've snapped centerlines and have used the 3-4-5 triangle to verify that they're perpendicular. Now it's time to figure out how much of a problem you might have, if any. To do this, measure from the squared-up reference line to the wall parallel to it, as illustrated in the drawing below. Do this at both ends of the reference line. In the example shown, the wall is out of square 1" for every 6 feet. In general, if the wall is out of square less than ¼" per 10 feet, you can make minor adjustments to the tiles that fit against the offending wall. For larger deviations you'll have to decide whether it's possible (and economical) to fix the wall, or whether you can live with obviously tapered tiles. If you go with tapered tiles, see page 59.

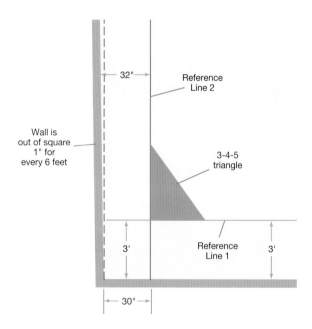

32"

Reference
Line 2

Wall is
out of square
1" for
every 6 feet

3-4-5
triangle

3'

Reference
Line 1

3'

30"

Making Major Adjustments

In most cases where a room is considerably out of square, it's not economically feasible to fix the offending wall or walls. This means you'll need to try to hide the variation as much as possible. One way to do this is to split the taper in two, as illustrated in the drawing below. Alternatively, look for areas where the taper won't be as noticeable, such as next to a built-in or, if you're installing tile flooring, under the toekick of a cabinet.

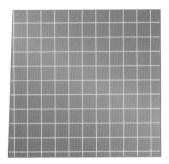

INCORRECT:
Tapered tiles
are obvious

CORRECT:
Tapered tiles are
less noticeable

Laying Out a Diagonal Floor

One of the best ways to make a floor more interesting is to install the tile on diagonals instead of parallel to the walls. A diagonal layout can also make a small space—like a galley kitchen—look larger. Laying out a diagonal floor is time-consuming, but straightforward.

1 SNAP CENTERED LINES. To lay out a floor on diagonals, start by locating and snapping a pair of centered lines. Make sure to use the 3-4-5 triangle described on page 55 to ensure that these lines are perpendicular to each other. Next, test the pattern by laying out tiles on these lines so their corners bisect these lines. If necessary, shift the reference lines to ensure equal partial tiles at the walls.

2 MARK EQUIDISTANT FROM CENTER. Next, use a tape measure or straightedge to measure and mark points equidistant from the centerpoint to match the width of the tile plus grout line (page 10). Do this along the full length of each reference line.

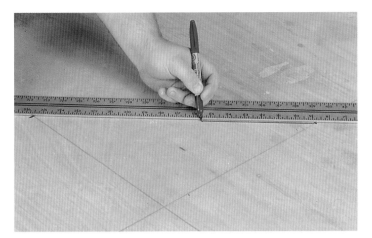

3 CONNECT THE DOTS. Now you can use a straightedge to connect the dots you just marked on the reference lines, as shown in the top photo. Do this for all four reference lines to create a square.

4 MARK THE REMAINDER OF THE GRID. Once you've drawn the first square, continue connecting the dots as you move away from the centerpoint, as shown in the bottom photo. As the lines lengthen, switch over to a chalk line (page 39). Before you tile, it's a good idea to once more lay down tile to check your pattern and adjust spacing as needed.

Laying Out Walls

Tiled walls that are out of plumb can be quite noticeable. That's why it's important to start with plumb reference lines, as described below. Also, in many cases you'll be using some sort of cove base to serve as a transition from wall to floor. Since cove base should always be installed as full tiles, you need to locate a baseline for installing the field tiles as described below. Finally, if you're tiling a tub surround, see the recommended layout sequence on page 63.

DRAW LEVEL AND PLUMB REFERENCE LINES. Chances are that your walls aren't plumb. So when you go to lay out a tile pattern on a wall, it's important to use a level to create a plumb reference line (as illustrated in the drawing at right) instead of measuring out from the adjacent walls—if you do this, you'll only duplicate the out-of-plumb problem instead of resolving it.

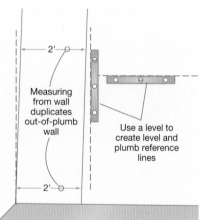

2'

Measuring from wall duplicates out-of-plumb wall

Use a level to create level and plumb reference lines

2'

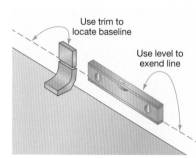

Use trim to locate baseline

Use level to exend line

LOCATING A BASELINE. If you'll be installing cove between the wall and floor or floor tile, you'll want to establish a baseline that will allow for full cove tiles, as illustrated in the bottom drawing.

SEQUENCE FOR TUB SURROUND. Laying out a surround for a tub requires a lot of forethought and planning. That's because the tile typically stops short of the ceiling and only extends just past the tub, as illustrated in the drawing below. Why all the planning? You'll want to locate the trim tiles that frame the field tiles so that you can plan the location of both the trim and field tiles. A story stick (page 131) is an invaluable layout tool for positioning your reference lines. Once you've located your outside reference lines (marked 1 and 2 in the drawing), use these to connect the sides to the back of the surround, as shown.

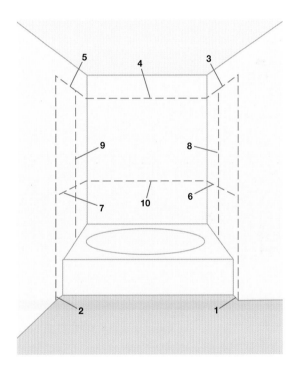

TILE KNOW-HOW

Laying Out a Countertop

Countertops tend to be easier to lay out than walls and floors because they're usually smaller and easier to work with, in terms of compensating for out-of-square and out-of-plumb problems.

FULL TILES AT FRONT EDGE. The most important rule for laying out a countertop is to use full field tiles at the front of the countertop. If you do have to install partial tiles, these should be installed along the back edge, where they'll be less noticeable, as illustrated in the middle drawing. This means you always tile from the front edge toward the back on a countertop. It also means you'll have to compensate for counter edging or other trim tile in your layout, as described on pages 154 and 167. See the opposite page for common layouts for a variety of countertop shapes.

Partial tiles
at backsplash

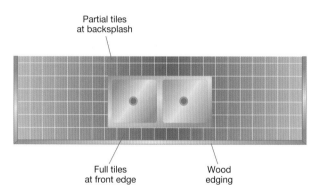

Full tiles
at front edge

Wood
edging

Tapered tiles at backsplash
caused by uneven wall

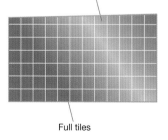

Full tiles

FITTING A COUNTERTOP TO AN UNEVEN WALL. If the wall that the countertop butts up against is uneven, you'll want any tapered partial tiles to be along this back edge, as illustrated in the bottom drawing. If you end up with narrow, tapered tiles, consider hiding them completely with a wider backsplash, like the bullnose version described on pages 164–165.

Regardless of the shape of a countertop, you'll need to locate and draw layout lines for your edging tiles, as illustrated in the drawing below. When possible, shift the reference lines to create full tiles around the sink opening. If this isn't possible, adjust the lines to create equal-width partial tiles on both sides of the sink. For more on this, see page 156.

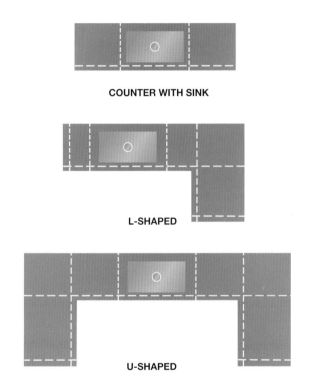

COUNTER WITH SINK

L-SHAPED

U-SHAPED

Laying Out Partial Tiles

A partial tile is any tile that's not a full or field tile and has been cut to fit around an obstacle such as a pipe or closet flange, or to fit against an edge or around a corner.

Working around obstacles

When you need to tile around an obstacle like a pipe, your first order of business is to transfer the obstacle location to your tile (see the photos below). Once you've located and marked the obstacle on the tile, you'll need to remove material so the tile can wrap around the obstacle. This may mean cutting holes (see page 95) or nibbling away a portion of the tile (see pages 93–94.)

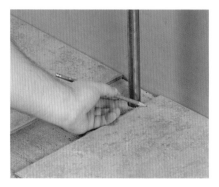

1 MAKE REFERENCE MARKS. The simplest way to transfer an obstacle onto a tile is to butt the tile up against the obstacle and make a reference mark, as shown. Make marks on both adjacent edges (note whether the tile is an edge tile and needs to be cut to fit; do this first, as described on page 67).

2 CONNECT MARKS TO LOCATE OBSTACLE. Now use a combination square or try square to connect the marks and locate the center-point of the obstacle, as shown.

EDGE TILES. To mark an edge tile, place a tile on the full tile nearest to the wall. Then set a ⅛" spacer against the wall and place a "marker" tile on top of the tile to be cut, as illustrated in the top drawing. Slide the marker tile until it butts against the spacer. Next, draw a line on the tile, using the edge of the marker tile as a guide. Now you'll get an accurate fit when you cut the bottom tile.

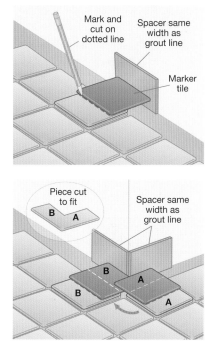

Mark and cut on dotted line

Spacer same width as grout line

Marker tile

Piece cut to fit

Spacer same width as grout line

CORNER TILES. Tile is linear; corners aren't. So it's tricky to produce partial tiles when you need to cut a notch to fit around a corner or other obstacle. The technique stays fairly constant: Use the same procedure to mark the tile as described above.

Here, though, you have to set up and mark the tile on both sides of the corner. Remember to insert a spacer between the wall and the tile equal to the thickness of one grout line.

Paper Templates

Want a foolproof way to guarantee that a partial tile will fit? Make a paper template first and then use this as a pattern to lay out the tile. Stiff paper like builder's red rosin paper or construction paper works best for this. Use the techniques described on pages 66–67 to create the paper template. Then check the fit. If everything looks good, use the template to transfer the pattern onto your tile.

Floor Preparation

Before you can tile a floor, you'll need to prep it so the adhesive will bond properly. There are different prep routines for concrete, existing vinyl, and ceramic floors.

Concrete

When you tile over concrete, odds are that it'll be cracked and in need of repair. If the cracks are less than ³⁄₈" wide, you can fix them yourself with some concrete patch. Cracks larger than this are best left to a professional.

1 FIX CRACKS. To repair cracked concrete, chip away any loose areas and use a wire brush to clean out the crack. Next, apply a concrete patch. These come in squeeze tubes and standard caulk tube formats. Use a pointer or trowel to feather the patch away from the edge to create a smooth surface.

2 CHECK FOR MOISTURE. Before you tile over concrete, it's important to do a moisture test to make sure excess moisture isn't wicking up through the concrete. To do this, cut a couple of 2-foot squares of plastic and duct tape them to various areas. Wait 72 hours. If you find beads of moisture on the underside of the plastic, you've got a moisture problem—call in a flooring contractor for advice. If the plastic is dry, you're good to go.

3 CHECK THE ABSORPTION. As a general rule, concrete makes an excellent foundation for tile. The one exception: concrete that's been treated with a curing, acceleration, or form-release compound. Any of these chemicals will prevent your adhesive from bonding to the concrete. To check for this, spray water on the slab; if the water absorbs, it's okay to tile.

Self-Leveling Compounds

If you're tiling a concrete slab, it may need leveling. In days past this meant calling in a skilled mason to float a level bed of mortar. But with the advent of self-leveling compounds (see page 33), anyone can quickly and easily level a concrete floor.

1 POUR OUT THE MIXTURE. Follow the manufacturer's directions to mix the compound. Exact measurements are critical here for the compounds to flow and set up properly, so measure carefully. Once it's

mixed, simply pour the compound into the low area and it will find its own level. Note: Make sure to block off areas where you don't want the compound to flow—a coil of plumber's putty works great for this since it's easily removed once the compound has cured.

2 SPREAD IF NEC-ESSARY. You may find that the leveling compound needs a little help to flow into some areas. So use a margin trowel or pointer to push or drag the material around as needed.

Vinyl

You can tile directly over an existing vinyl floor as long as it meets two conditions: It's firmly attached to the underlying surface, and it's scuffed up as described below to give the tile adhesive something to "bite" into.

1 SCUFF THE VINYL. Vinyl is too smooth to provide a good grip for tile adhesive, so rough up the surface with a coarse-grit sandpaper (80-grit). Use a sanding block (as shown) and sand in a circular motion.

2 REMOVE THE DUST. When you've sanded the entire vinyl floor, go back over it with a vacuum to remove all of the sanding dust and debris, as shown. Then vacuum it again to make sure it's clean.

Ceramic

Yes, you can tile directly over an existing ceramic floor, but it, too, must be firmly attached to its underlying surface. Make sure it's clean (see below), and note that you'll have to compensate for the added thickness of the new tile at thresholds and fixtures such as toilets. (For more on dealing with height variations at toilets, see page 107.)

CLEAN THOROUGHLY. An existing tile floor must be super-clean to have your tile adhesive stick well. Consider using a professional-strength tile cleaner, and rinse the floor thoroughly after cleaning before you tile.

Installing Plywood Underlayment

Installing plywood underlayment is a great way to create a flat reference surface for your new tile floor. It's fairly quick work, and there are only a few things to be aware of. First, make sure that the subfloor is level and that there are no dips (see page 54); level these as needed with a self-leveling compound, as described on page 69. Second, to prevent cracks in the new flooring, it's important that the seams of the underlayment don't align with the seams in the subfloor. Cut the underlayment as necessary to prevent this.

INSTALL THE SHEETS. To install new underlayment, begin by fastening sheets in one corner and work your way across the room. Cut sheets as necessary to prevent overlapping the seams in the sub-

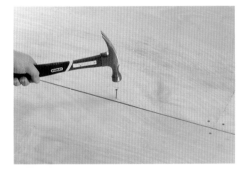

floor. Fasten the underlayment to the subfloor every 6" or so along the edges and at around 8" to 12" intervals throughout the sheet. Use 1"-long screws or ring-shank nails (as shown here).

SEAL THE JOINTS. To complete the underlayment, mix up some patching compound (or use thin-set) and spread it over the seams with a putty knife, as shown. After the compound is dry, scrape off the excess with a sharp putty knife.

TILE KNOW-HOW

Installing Backer Board

Backer board is rigid and stable, even when wet. That's the good news. The not-so-good news is that it can be expensive, heavy, and sometimes hard to work with (see below). But it is one of the best choices as an underlayment for tile. There are two main types of backer board available: cement board and fiber-based cement board, sold under the brand names WonderBoard and Hardiebacker, respectively. Both types rest on a bed of thin-set and are attached to the subfloor with galvanized screws or nails. See pages 76–77 for instructions on how to cut and drill backer board.

1 APPLY THIN-SET MORTAR. To install backer board, first mix thin-set mortar according to the manufacturer's instructions. Then, starting along the longest wall, apply the mortar with a notched trowel. Spread only enough mortar for one sheet at a time.

2 SECURE TO THE SUBFLOOR. Place a sheet on the thin-set and secure it to the subfloor with 1½" galvanized screws or nails every 6" or so along the edges and about every 8" throughout the rest of the sheet, as shown. Drive the fasteners in so they're slightly below the surface of the board. Continue like this, working along the wall or floor; then start the next row, making sure the end seams are offset and that you've left room for expansion joints as described on page 73.

3 EXPANSION JOINTS. As you lay successive sheets of backer board, it's important to set aside some room between sheets for expansion. A simple way to do this is to temporarily insert galvanized roofing nails between sheets to set the gap, as shown here. Once the sheets are fastened, these can be removed.

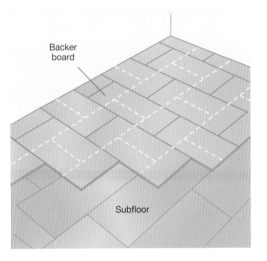

Backer board

Subfloor

4 STAGGER SHEETS. To prevent cracks in your new tile floor, the seams of the backer board should not match up with the seams in the subfloor, as illustrated in the bottom drawing. Cut the backer board as necessary to prevent this.

5 **APPLY FIBERGLASS TAPE.** When all the backer board is down, your final task is to cover the seams. To do this, first apply fiberglass mesh tape (page 35) over the seams as shown, taking care not to overlap any of the ends.

6 **SEAL THE JOINT.** Next, spread a layer of thin-set mortar over the tape with a putty knife, as shown. Feather the edges away from the seams to create a smooth surface. Allow the mortar to cure before laying tile.

No-Tape Backer Board

One of the big advantages that cement board offers over fiber-based backer board is the mesh tape that is embedded in the surface and also wraps around the edges, as shown in the photo below. Because the edges already have mesh tape to provide a purchase for thin-set, you don't have to tape the seams before applying the thin-set.

Attaching backer board to walls

Although backer board is most commonly attached to flooring, it also makes an excellent base for wall tile. Because there's less force applied to a wall than to a floor, thinner backer board can be used—¼" works great for this.

1 LOCATE AND MARK STUDS. Unlike a floor, where you've got the entire subfloor to fasten the backer board to, on walls the only solid purchase for fasteners is the wall studs and the top and bottom plate. So your first step is to locate and mark the framing members, as shown in the top photo.

2 POSITION AND SECURE. In many installations, the backer board can be attached to the wall studs without first applying a layer of thin-set. If you do want to apply thin-set first, make sure that the surface can handle it—exterior-rated plywood is fine, as well as moisture-resistant drywall. Steer clear of standard drywall, since the moisture in the adhesive can seep into the drywall and damage it. Attach the backer board to the wall studs every 6" or so, using 2"-long galvanized nails or screws.

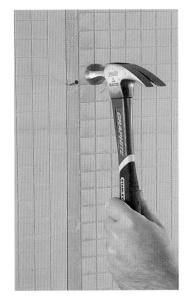

Cutting and Drilling Backer Board

Backer board can be cut by scoring and snapping (see below) or cut with a power saw fitted with a masonry blade.

1 SCORE THE CUT LINE. You can make straight cuts on both WonderBoard and Hardiebacker in a way similar to cutting drywall. Start by marking the cut line. Then score the line with a sharp utility knife (cutting this abrasive stuff will dull it quickly). Better yet, use a special carbide-tipped scorer designed especially for this (top right photo). Make a series of passes to deepen the cut.

2 SNAP THE BOARD. Now slide the board on your work surface so the scored line is at the edge, and press down to snap the board (or slip a 2×4 or dowel under the score line, as shown here). Hardiebacker will break off cleanly; with WonderBoard you'll generally need to cut though the mesh on the opposite face with a utility knife.

POWER SAW. Backer board can also be cut with a power saw fitted with a masonry blade. Why cut it when you can snap it? There are a few cases where cutting with a power saw is easier than scoring and snapping: partial cuts and thin strips. To snap a partial cut, you need to cut fully through the backer board to snap it. This is a chore by hand—but easy with a power saw. Although scoring a snap line for a thin strip is simple, it's hard to snap without breaking the strip. But a power saw can do this with ease—especially if fitted with a rip fence.

Drilling in Backer Board

Just as with tile, you can drill holes in backer board with masonry bits, glass and tile bits, and diamond hole saws (page 43). But you may not have these on hand or have the right size. If you have a small masonry bit and some black pipe, you can use the technique described here to "drill" almost any size hole. The only requirement is that you have a piece of black pipe that's the size of the hole you need.

1 **DRILL A SERIES OF HOLES.** Start by laying out the hole on the backer board. Then drill a series of holes around the perimeter, as shown.

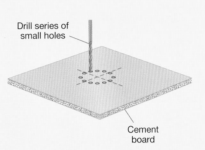

Drill series of small holes

Cement board

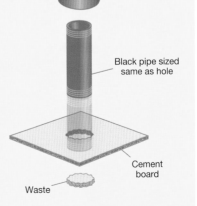

2 **PUNCH OUT WASTE WITH PIPE.** All that's left is to punch out the hole with a piece of black pipe and a hammer, as shown.

Black pipe sized same as hole

Cement board

Waste

Wall Preparation

Walls can be tiled directly if you first prepare the surface. How you do this depends on the existing wall covering.

Wallpaper

Many newer wallpapers are "strippable." That is, they can literally be peeled off the walls. Older, pasted-on wallpapers are removed by first breaking down the glue (see below).

1 PERFORATE THE PAPER. You may not need to perforate the wallpaper before spraying on a removal solution—it depends on whether the paper is porous. To test this, wet the paper with a sponge. If the water soaks in, you don't need to perforate. If it doesn't, the paper is coated and needs perforating. This entails punching tiny holes in the wallpaper with the aid of a perforating tool (often called by the brand name PaperTiger).

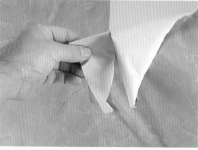

2 APPLY STRIPPER AND PEEL OFF. A garden sprayer works great to apply the removal solution. Follow the mixing instructions and fill the sprayer. Spray on generously, wait 15 minutes, and spray again. If the solution has done its work, the paper will peel right off as shown. If it doesn't, spray on additional coats. When the paper is removed, wash the wall with clean water to remove any adhesive residue.

Painted walls

The first step in prepping a painted wall is to clean it. You can quickly strip off dirt and grime by scrubbing a wall lightly with a sponge or brush saturated with a cleaning solution like trisodium phosphate (TSP). Just make sure to rinse the wall completely with clean water when done. If the existing paint is anything but flat, scuff the surface (see below).

1 **SCUFF GLOSSY FINISHES.** Any paint other than flat (satin, eggshell, semi-gloss, gloss) needs to be scuffed to provide something for the tile adhesive to grip. Fit a sanding block with 80-grit open-coat sandpaper, and sand in a circular motion. Change the paper frequently to keep it from clogging.

2 **REMOVE THE SANDING DUST.** When you're done sanding, go over the wall with a vacuum to remove any sanding dust and grit. Repeat a second time to thoroughly clean the surface.

Installing Membranes

As discussed on pages 15 and 34, a membrane serves to prevent moisture from wicking through grout and damaging the underlayment and/or framing. In order for the membrane to do its job, it must be installed properly. We'll cover how to install two of the most popular waterproofing membranes: sheet membranes and tar paper.

Sheet membrane

Sheet membranes do a terrific job of stopping moisture. They typically come in 5-foot widths and so are perfect for tub and shower surrounds. Because you install this type of membrane as a single sheet, it can be awkward to work with, so a helper is invaluable.

1 APPLY THIN-SET. Sheet membranes are sandwiched between the underlayment (backer board, or moisture-resistant drywall as shown here) and the tile. Some can be stapled to the underlayment (like 4-mil plastic and tar paper), but others are bonded to the underlayment with thin-set mortar. Apply the thin-set with a small V-notch trowel.

2 POSITION THE MEMBRANE. Position the cut end of the membrane a couple of inches past the thin-set, and begin to roll out the membrane. Take care to keep the roll plumb so that it will roll out evenly.

3 EXTEND ALONG THE WALL. Continue rolling out the membrane, making sure that its top edge is level. What you're doing here is roughly positioning the membrane so that it can be pressed in place and trimmed as needed.

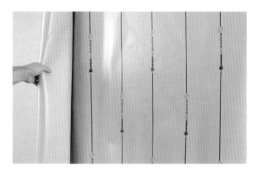

4 USE A ROLLER TO SET THE SHEET. Start in the middle of the membrane and work your way out toward its edges, pressing the membrane into the thin-set with a roller. A laminate roller works great for this, but a rolling pin can also be pressed into service. Starting in the center allows you to push trapped air out toward the ends. Repeat for the other half.

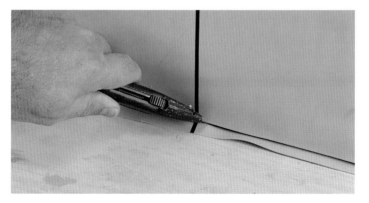

5 TRIM AS NEEDED. Once the membrane is secured by the adhesive, you can work around the perimeter, trimming it to fit as shown.

Tar paper

Tar paper is favored among pros because it's both inexpensive and easy to install.

1 ROLL OUT THE PAPER.
To make the tar paper more manageable, first measure the area to be covered, add 10%, and cut a sheet to length. Then start by extending one end a few inches past the start point and begin unrolling the paper, as shown.

2 SECURE WITH STAPLES.
Secure the tar paper as you go, with ½" staples spaced about every 6" to 8" in the field and every 4" to 6" around the perimeter.

3 OVERLAP LAYERS.
Since tar paper comes in standard lengths of 36", you'll need to use multiple sheets to cover a wider area—like the average tub or shower surround. Upper layers of tar paper should always overlap the lower layers by at least 2"—more if you've got plenty of excess.

Mixing Adhesives and Grout

Mixing adhesives and grout, although tedious, is fairly straightforward. Make sure to read and follow the manufacturer's directions since they vary from material to material and from one maker to the next.

1 ADD WATER TO DRY MIX. Depending on your material, you'll add either water to mix, or the mix to water. On most, you add water to the mix. Make sure to use clean, cool water, and either measure the water as directed or add it slowly to the powder, stopping frequently to mix. For most adhesives and grouts, you're looking for an oatmeal-like consistency.

2 MIX WITH A PADDLE. Fit a corded drill with a mixing paddle (page 47) and push the paddle down into the bottom of your bucket. Turn on power and "stir" the mix with the paddle, moving it in a circular motion. Stop frequently to check the consistency, and add water as needed.

(page 47)

PRO TIP

Clean Tools Immediately

If left to dry on your tools, grout and especially thin-set can set up and be very tough to remove. That's why pros always clean their tools immediately after use. This includes paddles, buckets, sponges, trowels, and floats.

TILE KNOW-HOW

Spreading Adhesives

For the most part, adhesives—both thin-set and mastics—are spread on underlayment with some sort of notched trowel. The type and size of the trowel you'll use depends on the size of the tile you're laying (see page 46 for more on this).

WORK IN SMALL AREAS. The number one rule for successfully working with adhesives is to work in small areas. The smaller the notch on your trowel, the smaller this area should be, since small ridges of adhesive

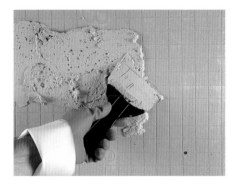

tend to dry out and set up more quickly than larger ridges. For wall tile, a 2- to 3-foot-square area is about as large as you should work. With floor tile you can generally work larger areas. Since it can be difficult to fit a trowel in a bucket, you may find it easier to lift the adhesive out and apply it to the wall with a putty knife, as shown in the top photo.

FLATTEN TROWEL TO SPREAD. To apply adhesive to underlayment, keep the trowel fairly flat to spread the adhesive broadly over the area. You're not using the notches here; what you're trying to do is spread an even foundation layer.

TILT TROWEL TO USE NOTCHES. Once you have your working area mostly covered with adhesive, tilt the trowel to about 45 degrees and pull or push the notched edge through the adhesive, as shown. It's important to keep the trowel at the same relative angle to create ridges that are identical in height. In tight areas, switch to the notched end of the trowel.

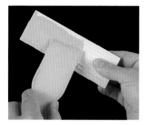

BACK-BUTTERING. In areas with restricted access, or when dealing with small tiles or trim tiles, you may find it easier to apply the adhesive to the tile and not to the underlayment. This technique is called back-buttering because it's similar to buttering a piece of toast. The key thing here is to apply a uniformly thick layer of adhesive. A putty knife or a notched margin trowel (page 47), with its small size, is an excellent tool for this job.

(page 47)

P R O   T I P

Check Coverage Frequently

If you've ever watched pros tile a floor, you've seen them periodically stop and pull up a tile they've just laid and look at the back of the tile. They haven't made a mistake. Instead, they're checking the coverage of the adhesive. What they're generally looking for is at minimum 80% to 90% of the tile covered with adhesive. If they're not getting that much coverage, they'll either apply more adhesive or set the tiles deeper into the adhesive—or both.

TILE KNOW-HOW

REMOVE EXCESS ADHESIVE.
The best time to remove any excess adhesive that may have squeezed out into the gaps between the tiles is right after you've set your tiles (pages 86–89). If you allow thin-set to dry, you'll have to scrape it out to prevent it from interfering with the grout. Since most thin-set is gray, and grout is frequently light in color, excess thin-set will look bad if left to harden between the tiles. A dental pick (as shown

here) works great to clean out narrow grout lines; the edge of a putty knife works well for wider grout lines.

WORKING WITH ORGANIC MASTICS

If you're going to use a solvent-based organic mastic, you'll need to take some extra safety precautions. As a general rule, solvent-based mastics tend to irritate skin, so it's always a good idea to wear rubber gloves. Also, solvent-based organic mastics should be used only with adequate ventilation to prevent irritating lungs. If this isn't possible, make sure to wear a respirator with charcoal cartridges. You can always tell whether or not a charcoal cartridge is working. If you can't smell the mastic, it's working; if you can, it isn't.

Setting Tile

Setting tile is the fun part of tile projects. After all the preparation and layout, you finally get to see the fruits of your labors. There are two steps to setting tile: positioning tile, and setting it into the adhesive.

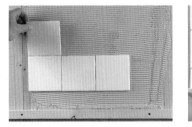

FIELD AND PARTIAL TILES. Generally, field tiles are placed first. The exceptions to this are when the area you're tiling will be framed in trim tile (like the tub surround on pages 133–140), or when you're tiling a countertop (see pages 152–159). To place a tile, try to set it directly onto the thin-set to keep from shifting the adhesive to one side or the other. Once it's on the adhesive, twist the tile as you press down to spread the adhesive. Once all your field tiles are in place, cut and install any partials.

PRO TIP

Mixing Tiles

When professional painters take on a big job that requires multiple buckets of same-color paint, they'll always intermix paint from one can to another to blend color variations from can to can. Pro tilers do the same thing when they mix tiles from carton to carton. This not only helps with color but also blends any discrepancies in pattern and texture from carton to carton.

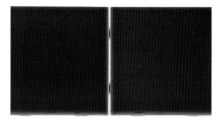

BUILT-IN SPACERS.

Small tiles—particularly ceramic tile used for walls and countertops— typically have built-in spacers to set the gaps between the tiles. These spacers are small tabs that protrude from the edges of the tile. If you press two tiles together and hold them up to a light, they're easy to see (top photo). In use, you simply butt the tiles up against each other, and spacing is automatic. What's particularly nice about built-in spacers is that unlike rubber spacers (see below), they don't have to be removed prior to grouting.

P R O T I P

Using Spacers Correctly

When you look at a cross-shaped rubber spacer, you might logically assume that the spacer is laid down flat at the corner of a tile to set the gap for grout. Not so. Instead, rubber spacers should be positioned vertically, as shown. This way they're easy to remove before grouting. If you lay them flat, you'll probably have to pry them out. Not only can this take a lot of time, especially on a large tile job, but prying out spacers can also chip off corners and crack tile.

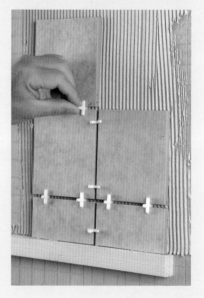

REMOVING FLAT SPACERS. If you do inadvertently install a rubber spacer wrong and the adhesive has dried, you'll have to pry it out carefully. Using a dental pick like the one shown here is an excellent way to hook onto the end of the spacer so that you can gently pull it out.

Leveling with a Caul

Although you can set tile one tile at a time with a rubber mallet, it's time-consuming and doesn't help level tile to tile. A more efficient method is to make a caul like the one shown here.

It's just a length of 2×4 wrapped with a scrap of carpet to provide cushioning. To use, place the caul across the tiles at a diagonal and tap it near its center a couple of times with a rubber mallet or hammer. This not only sets the tiles, but also levels them from tile to tile.

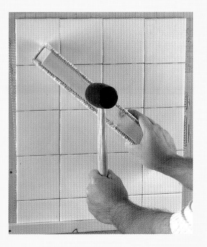

TILE KNOW-HOW

Cutting Tile

Tile can be cut in various ways: with a snap cutter or handheld snap cutter, with a motorized wet saw, or with a tile nipper. Which tool you use will depend on the material you're cutting and the type of cut you're making.

Snap cutter

When you need to make a straight cut on a flat tile—particularly ceramic tile—a snap cutter (page 41) is the tool for the job. Some hard materials, like porcelain and glass, are best cut with a motorized wet saw (page 92).

1 MARK THE CUT LINE. To cut a tile using a snap cutter, start by marking the cut line on the tile with a square and a permanent marker.

2 POSITION THE TILE IN THE CUTTER. Next, lift up the sliding arm on the snap cutter and position the tile in the cutter so the mark you just made is aligned with the cutting wheel on the sliding arm.

3 SCORE THE TILE. To score the tile, slide the arm across the tile while pressing down. This doesn't take a lot of pressure, as long as the wheel is sharp. What's important, though, is that you score the line in a single pass. Multiple scored lines tend to result in uneven edges when the tile is snapped.

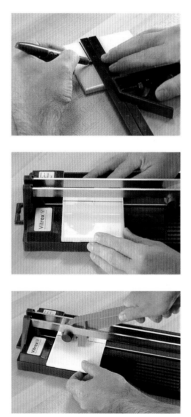

4 SNAP THE TILE. To snap the tile at the scored line, just lift the sliding arm up so its wings rest on the tile on both sides of the scored line. Then press down firmly to snap the tile. If it doesn't snap right away, try tapping the end of the arm abruptly with a closed fist. This will usually get the job done.

Handheld snap cutter

A handheld snap cutter combines a scoring wheel and snapping wings in one portable tool.

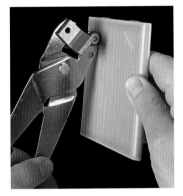

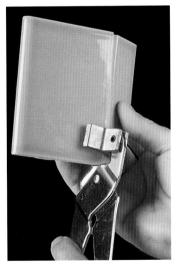

1 SCORE THE TILE. Although you can score a tile freehand (as shown here), if you're after a straight cut, you should use some kind of straightedge to guide the cutting wheel.

2 SQUEEZE TO SNAP. Once you've scored the tile, just open the jaws of the tool and insert the tile so the wings span the scored line. Then squeeze the handle to snap the tile.

Motorized wet saw

Some hard materials like porcelain and glass are best cut with a motorized wet saw fitted with a diamond blade. Although wet saws are primarily used to make straight cuts, when making complex cuts in all types of tile, they're extremely useful for cutting partial tiles and removing waste.

SET UP A WORK SPACE. Motorized wet saws are messy, so it's best to set them up outdoors. To prevent back fatigue, place the saw on a work surface that lets you make a cut without stooping over. And because water is involved, make sure that you plug the saw into a GFCI-protected receptacle. A ground-fault circuit interruptor will prevent a nasty shock if you mix electricity with water. Have a hose handy to fill up the saw's reservoir and clean rags on hand to mop up spills and to dry tiles.

CUTTING WITH A RIP FENCE. Most saws come with a rip fence that snaps in place. Set its position by measuring from the fence to the blade. Turn on the saw and make the cut, pressing the tile firmly against the fence as you guide it into the blade. Firm, gentle pressure is all that's needed here.

CUTTING WITH A MITER GAUGE. Some saws come with a separate miter gauge or one that fits over the rip fence (as shown here) to make angled or straight cuts in tile. To use a miter gauge, hold the tile against the gauge and guide it along the fence, pushing the tile into the blade as shown.

Complex cuts

Complex cuts—where a portion of the tile has to be removed to fit around an obstacle—are easily made with the help of a motorized wet saw.

CUTTING NOTCHES IN TILE. Tile often needs to be notched to fit around the corner of a wall. The notch is usually cut by making two intersecting cuts, as shown. When you do this, make sure that the waste portion of the tile is not against the fence on the second cut. If it is, it can be trapped between the blade and the rip fence and can kick back.

REMOVING EXCESS TILE. When you need to make a complex cut that's curved, you can save yourself a lot of time nibbling (see page 94) if you remove as much waste as possible (as shown here) and then cut slots (see below).

CUTTING SLOTS. Although you can use tile nippers (page 94) without first cutting slots in the waste portion of a complex cut, it's much easier going if you do cut slots. Cutting slots in the waste does two things: It removes material and creates fracture points for the nippers, which help prevent it from nipping into the good portion of the tile (for more on this, see page 94).

Using Tile Nippers

Tile nippers or "biters" are the primary tool for cutting curves in tile. They're easy to use and fairly efficient. Their only drawback: They can sometimes be hard to control, and they almost always leave a ragged edge. That's because they break off pieces of tile instead of making a controlled cut as with a snap cutter or wet saw.

1 REMOVE THE BULK OF THE WASTE. To use a tile nipper, first mark the curve on the tile. Then open the jaws of the nipper and insert the tile. Squeeze the handle to close the jaws and break off a piece of tile. To better control how the tile breaks, consider cutting a series of slots in the waste area of the tile, as described on page 93. Cutting slots like this makes it easy for the nippers to snap off small chucks, as shown in the top photo.

2 FINE-TUNE THE SHAPE. Once you've removed the bulk of the waste, go back around the perimeter of the profile, taking smaller bites until the desired shape is achieved. Just remember that the larger the piece you try to break off, the less control you'll have on the outcome. Small cuts may take longer, but you'll ruin fewer tiles.

Cutting Holes in Tile

M any tile jobs call for holes in tiles, most often to fit around plumbing pipes or fixtures. You'll also need holes in tile if you're planning on fastening a fixture (like a grab bar) to a tile wall. You can drill holes in tile with special bits (page 43) or cut the hole without a drill (see the sidebar below). If you drill the hole, make sure to use a centerpunch to create a starting point for the bit.

GLASS AND TILE BITS. Since glass and tile bits grind a hole instead of cutting one, they work better when lubricated. You can fashion a small moat for water with a coil of plumber's putty, as shown here. Add water, and drill with firm, gentle pressure.

DIAMOND HOLE SAWS. Like a glass and tile bit, a diamond hole saw will also cut better when lubricated. You can use the moat method described above or spray water on the bit with a spray bottle. Diamond hole saws work best when fitted in a drill press, but can also be used in a portable drill.

TILE KNOW-HOW

> **Q U I C K   F I X**
>
> ## Holes without Drills
>
> Want to cut a hole without drilling? Or need to cut a square hole? Try this trick. First cut the tile in half at the centerpoint of the hole. Then remove the waste by cutting a series of slots and nipping away the waste, as shown.

Grouting

Although grouting is easy to do, it's one of the messiest and most time-consuming tiling tasks. That's because you're basically smearing grout all over tile as you press it into the gaps between tiles. Then you have to remove all the excess.

1 ALLOW THE GROUT TO SLAKE. Once you've mixed your grout (page 83), the manufacturer's directions will probably instruct you to let the grout rest or "slake" a specific length of time. Slaking lets the dry ingredients be fully wetted by the water. When you've waited the specified time, give the grout another stir to remove any remaining lumps.

2 APPLY GROUT WITH A FLOAT. As when working with adhesives, it's best to work in small, manageable areas. Use your grout float to scoop out some grout and apply it to the tile as shown. Hold the float fairly flat to distribute the grout evenly over your work area.

3 **PRESS THE GROUT INTO THE GAPS.** Now tilt the float to use its edge to force grout into the gaps between the tiles, as shown. You can use either the side or end of the float to do this.

4 **SQUEEGEE OFF THE EXCESS.** After you've pressed grout into the gaps, hold the float at about 45 degrees to the surface of the tile and drag it diagonally across the tile as shown; this will squeegee off as much grout as possible. The more grout you get up with this technique, the less you'll have to sponge off later (page 98).

(page 98)

PRO TIP

Damp-Curing Grout

If you want to minimize grout's ability to absorb water while also maximizing its strength, consider damp-curing the grout. To do this, just mist the grout with water several times a day for two to three days after grouting. Make sure not to damp-cure tinted grout, as misting can dissolve the tint and produce inconsistent color.

TILE KNOW-HOW

5 CLEAN WITH A SPONGE.
Once you've removed the excess grout with the float used as a squeegee, it's time for the bucket and sponge. Wring out the sponge so it's barely damp, and wipe it across the grout lines at a diagonal, as shown. Wiping in line with the grout joints will pull the grout out of the gaps. Rinse the sponge frequently and replace the water often.

6 REMOVE THE HAZE.
Allow the grout to dry until it forms a haze on the tile. Then go over the tile with a clean, dry cloth to buff away the haze. Shake out the cloth frequently and change to a fresh cloth when it becomes soiled.

P R O   T I P

Sealing Grout

■▼■ Grout is porous and if
▶▲ not sealed will allow
moisture to seep through to the underlayment and framing. To prevent this, the grout needs to be sealed. But before you seal the grout, make absolutely sure it's dry. Otherwise, you'll be sealing in moisture, which can result in mold and mildew. Check the sealer's label for the recommended wait period. The minimum wait is usually 48 hours, but longer is required for damp or humid areas.

Using a Grout Bag

Grout bags offer pinpoint control when applying grout. They're particularly useful when grouting floors where large tiles have been used. By applying the grout directly to the gaps in the tile, you save time removing excess grout and cleaning the tile.

1 FILL THE BAG. To use a grout bag, fold over the edges at the open end to better support the bag, and fill the bag with grout, using a margin trowel or putty knife.

2 SQUEEZE TO DISPENSE. Unfold the end of the bag and twist it to force the grout down near the tip. Continue twisting and squeezing to dispense the grout into the gaps between the tiles, as shown.

3 TOOL THE JOINT. Unless you had perfect control when dispensing the grout, chances are it will need to be smoothed or "tooled." You can do this with a grout float (as shown here) or with a dowel, as described on page 107.

5

Tile Floors

WANT TO TRANSFORM the look of a room while also creating a durable surface that withstands heavy traffic? Then you want to tile a floor. A tiled floor is also impervious to most spills and is easy to clean and maintain. In this chapter, we'll show you how to lay standard floor tile, create a patterned floor, lay mosaic tile, tile over concrete, and install thresholds and baseboard. **Safety note:** Whatever tile you choose for a floor, make sure it has a textured surface to prevent slips.

Standard Floor Tiles

Because floors are subjected to a lot more stress than other tiled surfaces, it's especially important that you begin with a proper foundation. This means a sturdy, level subfloor of ¾" plywood or two layers of ⅝" plywood, topped by ½" cement board, as illustrated in the drawing below. The tile is set in a bed of thin-set mortar; the size of the notched trowel you'll use will depend on the size of the tile you're using (see page 46).

After you've chosen tile for your floor, you need to select the pattern you're going to use (see pages 8–10). One way to visualize what pattern will look best is to lay a row or two of tiles on the floor. Try a square pattern, or maybe one where the tiles are oriented diagonally to the corners of the room. Remember to leave space between the tiles roughly equivalent to the size of the grout joint you've chosen. Better yet, insert the actual spacers between the tiles as you lay them down.

Before you begin to lay tile, take the time to check that the floor is level (page 54). And, level it as needed (page 69). Then install the appropriate underlayment, as described on pages 72–74. Alternatively, if you'll be laying tile over existing flooring, see pages 68 and 70.

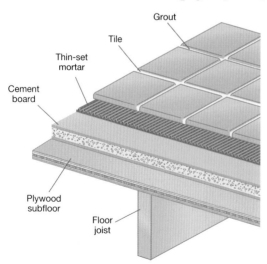

Grout

Tile

Thin-set mortar

Cement board

Plywood subfloor

Floor joist

1 **DRAW STARTING LINES.** The key to every successful floor tile installation is laying out the reference grid. Once you've established your pattern, begin by measuring and marking your first reference line (top photo). Use a framing square to establish a centered line perpendicular to the first line, and mark this. Adjust these lines as needed so your pattern produces equal partial tiles, as described on pages 56–57.

Trimming at Jambs

When tile meets the wood trim at a doorway, you have two options: You can cut the tile to fit around the molding, or trim the molding so the tile will fit under it. The easier of the two—and generally the better looking—is to trim the molding. To do this, lay a tile on the floor and use

this as a gauge to raise your handsaw to the correct height, as shown in the photo at left. Then saw through the molding and remove the waste.

TILE FLOORS

2 APPLY THE THIN-SET. Use a square-notched trowel to spread the thin-set mortar up to the reference lines you marked earlier. Avoid working the thin-set excessively. What you're looking for here is consistent ridges with no bare spots.

Tiling under Appliances

When tiling a kitchen floor, it's best to tile under the existing appliances. For pull-out appliances like a refrigerator and some ranges, this isn't a problem. But a built-in appliance, like a dishwasher, can be a real challenge. That's because there may not be sufficient clearance between the floor and countertop for the appliance with the added height of the tile. You have a couple of options here. One is not to tile under the dishwasher, but this will make it difficult to pull it out for servicing. Another is to shim the entire countertop higher. Or, if the countertop has a lip, you may be able to notch this to create sufficient clearance.

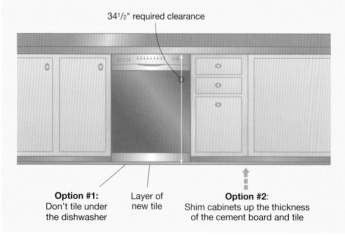

$34^1/_2$" required clearance

Option #1:
Don't tile under
the dishwasher

Layer of
new tile

Option #2:
Shim cabinets up the thickness
of the cement board and tile

3 POSITION THE FIELD TILES. Now you can begin to lay the field tiles. Start by positioning the first tile in the corner where the reference lines meet. Press down and twist slightly as you lay the tile to force it into the thin-set.

4 LAY ADDITIONAL TILES. Continue laying tiles along both reference lines. Once these are in place, continue to fill the entire area you're working. To ensure consistent spacing and even grout joints, insert tile spacers between the tiles as you go.

5 INSTALL ANY PARTIAL TILES. As you near a wall or obstruction, you'll have to stop laying full tiles and measure, mark, and cut partial tiles as needed. This can be as simple as cutting a narrow strip for edging (bottom photo), or as complex as cutting a series of curved tiles to fit around a closet flange, as shown in the upper left photo above. For more on laying out and cutting partial tiles, see pages 66–67 and pages 90–95, respectively.

COVE BASE ALTERNATIVES.

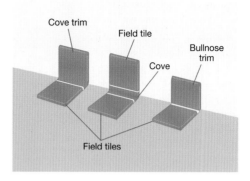

Cove trim

Field tile

Bullnose trim

Cove

Field tiles

Besides the actual pattern of your tile floor, another thing to plan ahead for is how you'll treat the transition from floor tile to wall. There are quite a few options here, including tile or wood baseboard and plastic cove base molding. Cove base molding and wood trim, as well as some tile baseboard (see pages 120–121), are installed after the floor is tiled and require little or no advance planning. Other tile baseboard options, like those illustrated in the drawing above, do require advance planning, as they often extend out into the floor area. Tile cove and bullnose trim are the simplest of the options, while individual cove pieces are more complicated to install.

P R O   T I P

No-Hassle Baseboard

When many homeowners tile an existing floor, they begin prepping the room by removing baseboards, only to find they need to install new baseboards once the tiling is complete. A no-hassle version of this is to leave the

baseboards in place. Then tile up to these, leaving the appropriate expansion gap. Next, cover the gap and create a smooth transition by simply adding a small piece of quarter-round shoe molding, as shown in the photo at left.

6 APPLY THE GROUT.
When the thin-set has dried overnight, you can grout. Using a grout float, spread the grout over the tiles and into the gaps between them. Press down firmly to force the grout into the joints. Then hold the float at an angle to squeegee off the excess.

7 TOOL THE GROUT. After you've sponged the tile clean (page 98), you may want to "tool" the grout lines to give them a uniform appearance. Although you can purchase a special tool for this, a scrap of dowel will do. To use a dowel, place it on a grout joint and draw it along the tile with gentle pressure.

P R O   T I P

Closet Flange Risers

When you tile a floor, you increase its thickness or height. In most cases, this isn't a problem. But in some cases—like where a toilet sits—it is. What you need is a spacer that will offset the additional height so the toilet can sit flat on the floor. That's the job of a closet flange riser (bottom photo). The riser rests on the flange, and the closet flange bolts pass through the toilet base and riser and into the closet flange. This firmly secures the toilet to the floor.

TILE FLOORS

Patterned Floor

In addition to color, texture, and pattern choices, there are additional ways you can add interest to any floor by either using a different layout pattern (like running bond—see below), or using different-shaped tile, like the hexagon tiles described on page 111. Although both are easy to install, they do require additional layout time.

Running-bond pattern

The standard pattern for flooring is stacked (see page 25), where all the tiles are aligned in straight rows. For added visual interest, consider the running-bond pattern described here. The running-bond pattern features rows of tiles offset by half a tile—a pattern commonly used for brickwork.

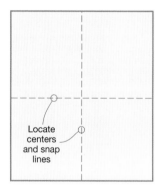

Locate centers and snap lines

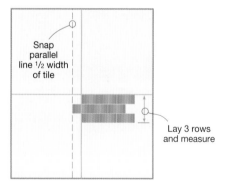

Snap parallel line 1/2 width of tile

Lay 3 rows and measure

1 SNAP CENTER-LINES. To lay out a running-bond pattern, start by snapping a pair of perpendicular lines centered on the room.

2 SNAP PATTERN LINES. Next, measure over from one of the reference lines the width of a tile plus half a grout line width and make a mark. Then snap a line at this mark parallel to the reference line.

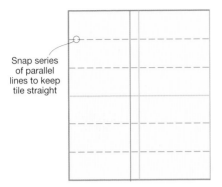

Snap series of parallel lines to keep tile straight

3 **RUNNING-BOND PATTERN.** Now lay down three rows of tile with spacers (but without mortar) and measure the combined height of the rows. Then measure, mark, and snap a series of parallel guide lines, as shown.

4 **DRY-TEST THE PATTERN.** Once you've snapped all your reference lines, take the time to once more dry-test your pattern. Lay down at least three rows to check the layout, as shown.

5 **APPLY THE THIN-SET.** If everything looks good, remove the tiles and mix up some thin-set mortar. Apply the thin-set to your underlayment with the appropriate-sized trowel (page 46). Spread the thin-

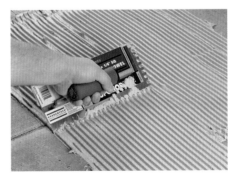

set up to the reference lines, taking care not to obscure them, as shown in the bottom photo. Apply sufficient thin-set to lay the first two rows of tile.

6 **LAY THE FIRST TWO ROWS.** Now you can begin laying tile. Start by positioning the first tile in the corner where the first set of reference lines meet. Press down and twist slightly as you lay the tile to force it into the thin-set. Insert spacers between

the tiles and continue laying tile with spacers offsetting the second row, until you've tiled the first two rows, as shown.

7 **APPLY MORE THIN-SET.** Continue now by applying thin-set for the next two rows, once again taking care not to obscure the reference lines you snapped earlier.

8 **CONTINUE WITH THE PATTERN.** Lay the next two rows of tile, inserting spacers between the tiles as you go. After you've got an area filled with tile, level the tiles with a shop-made caul as described on page 89. Slide the caul slowly across the tiles, working from one edge to the other. Overlap the caul onto the tiles adjacent to the first set you leveled and repeat the process. This is the simplest way to prevent the corner of a tile (or tiles) from protruding above

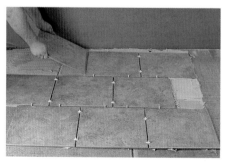

the others. Continue like this until you've tiled the entire floor, cutting and installing partial tiles as needed. Allow the thin-set to dry, and then grout (pages 96–99).

Laying out hex tile

Laying out hex tile is similar to laying out a running-bond pattern.

1 **LAY OUT TILES AND MEASURE.** Start by snapping perpendicular centered lines. Then lay four rows of tile with spacers and measure the combined distance.

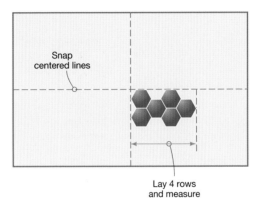

Snap
centered lines

Lay 4 rows
and measure

2 **SNAP A GRID.** Use this measurement to mark and snap a series of parallel lines to serve as a guide as you set the tile.

Snap parallel lines

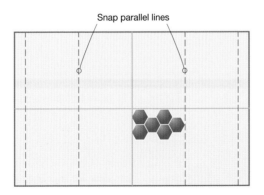

Mosaic Floor Tile

Mosaic tile isn't a pattern, it's a size: any tile 2" square or smaller. Most ceramic mosaic tiles are mounted on a backing sheet of rubber, plastic, or heavy thread that groups the tiles in sections for easier installation. You don't have to be concerned with tile spacing since it's already preset. All you have to take care of is the spacing between the tile sheets. You'll find mosaic tiles in 12"-square sheets in a variety of styles (illustration at right) and other sheet dimensions, depending on the design.

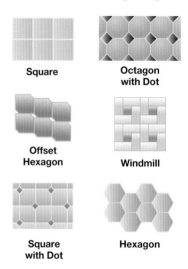

Square

Octagon with Dot

Offset Hexagon

Windmill

Square with Dot

Hexagon

Thanks to their small size, mosaic tiles fit well with contoured or irregular shapes—they can be wrapped around corners and obstacles. They are also easier to cut into partial tiles. You may not have to cut a tile at all: Just cut the backing sheet and remove a single tile.

1 DRY-TEST THE PATTERN. To install mosaic tile, start by measuring, marking, and snapping perpendicular centerlines on the floor. Then take the time to dry-test your pattern to make sure it'll work on the floor. Lay down sheets of mosaic, keeping the appropriate space between sheets to make sure there won't be any problems.

2 APPLY THIN-SET MORTAR. Check the manufacturer's recommendation for trowel notch size. As with other tiles, apply thin-set in about a 4-foot-square area at a time.

3 INSTALL THE FULL SHEETS. Because mosaic tiles have so many grout lines, a crooked tile pattern can be really noticeable. That's why just as with larger tile, you should work off reference lines to keep things straight. Install full sheets beginning at the reference lines, and continue to lay sheets to fill in your 4-foot-square area.

4 INSTALL PARTIAL SHEETS. Partial sheets should be installed once the full sheets are laid. Partial sheets may or may not need to be cut with a tile saw. Because of mosaics' size, sometimes all it takes to get a sheet to fit is to cut the backing and remove a tile or two.

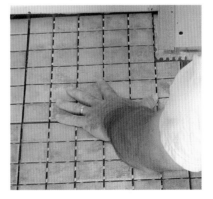

5 SET AND LEVEL THE TILES. Immediately after the sheets are laid, you should set or "bed" them in the mortar. This way, the mortar spreads evenly beneath the tile and gives the best possible grip. This is especially important with mosaic tiles, since you need to level the many, smaller tiles in a sheet. The best tool for the job is a soft rubber–faced mallet, or a "dead-blow" mallet; a closed fist will do in a pinch. A shop-made caul (page 89) does a great job of leveling tile from sheet to sheet. You're trying to spread the mortar on the back of the tile, not squeeze it out, so use multiple, light strikes. It's not time to grout yet: Once all the tiles are in place, let the mortar set up overnight, then grout.

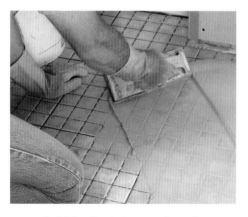

6 APPLY THE GROUT. There's a lot more grout involved in grouting mosaic tile than with standard tile. That's really the only difference of any note. Prepare just enough grout to work a 4- or 5-foot-square section of tile at a time. Apply the grout with a grout float, pushing the grout into the gaps between the tiles. Then hold the float at an angle and squeegee off the excess. Use a damp sponge to clean the tile. When the tile is dry, wipe off the haze with a clean cloth.

Tiling on Concrete

Concrete makes an excellent foundation for tile—as long as it's clean (see below), it's level, and there are no moisture problems (see page 68). The tile can be set in a thin or thick bed of mortar, as illustrated in the drawing at right. What's especially nice about tiling over concrete is that you don't need to install any backer board—the concrete is all the foundation you need. If the concrete is cracked, however, you may want to install an isolation membrane (page 34) between the concrete and the tile. This will prevent any shifting in the concrete from transferring to and damaging the tile.

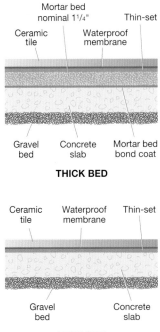

THICK BED

Mortar bed nominal 1¹/₄"   Thin-set
Ceramic tile   Waterproof membrane
Gravel bed   Concrete slab   Mortar bed bond coat

THIN-SET

Ceramic tile   Waterproof membrane   Thin-set
Gravel bed   Concrete slab

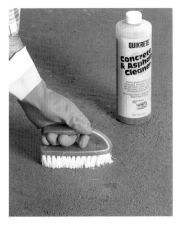

1 PREP THE CONCRETE. For thin-set to bond well to concrete, the concrete must be clean. Concrete cleaners are available for this and can be applied with an ordinary garden sprayer. Since these cleaners tend to be caustic, make sure to wear eye protection as well as rubber gloves when working with them. Let the concrete dry completely before proceeding. If the concrete surface is smooth, it should be roughed up with a hand grinder or power grinder to give the thin-set something to grip (make sure to wear eye protection when roughing up concrete).

2 TEST THE PATTERN. Once you've established the pattern you want and have snapped perpendicular center-lines, take the time to dry-test your pattern to make sure it'll work as planned. Remember to leave a space between the tiles roughly equivalent to the size of the grout joint you've chosen, or insert plastic tile spacers between the tiles as you lay them down.

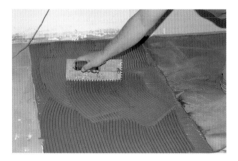

3 APPLY THE THIN-SET. Mix up enough thin-set mortar to cover about 4 square feet. Then use a square-notched trowel to spread the mortar on the concrete, as shown in the middle photo. Most thin-set mortar manufacturers suggest a ¼" to ⅜" notch for tiles 12" or less in length; larger tiles may require a ½" notch.

4 POSITION THE FIELD TILES. Start by setting a full tile along your reference line. Press down as you lay the tile to force it into the mortar, as shown in the bottom photo. As soon as the tile is down, "set" it in the mortar by tapping it with a soft rubber–faced mallet; this makes the mortar spread evenly to give the best grip possible. Continue laying tiles along the reference line. To ensure consistent spacing, use plastic tile spacers between each tile.

5 **INSTALL ANY PARTIAL TILES.**
Partial tiles can be installed once the full tiles have been laid and set (top photo). A partial tile is any tile that's not a full tile and has been cut to

fit around an outside corner or other obstacle, such as a closet flange. For more on marking and cutting partial tiles, see pages 66–67 and 90–95, respectively.

6 **SET THE TILE.**
Even if your floor is level, you'll often come across a tile that doesn't sit level on the floor. In situations like these, apply a dollop or two of thin-set mortar to the

low areas, as shown in the middle photo. Replace the tile and check for level; add or remove mortar as needed. Once all the tiles are in place, let the mortar set up overnight.

7 **APPLY THE GROUT.** Before you apply grout, remove any plastic spacers. Mix up only enough grout to work a small section of tile at a time. This not only lets you take

your time to do the job right, but it also makes mixing easier, since you're working with smaller batches. Start in a corner and pour some grout on the tile. Use a grout float to force the grout into the joints, as shown in the bottom photo. Remove excess grout and clean the tile as described on pages 96–98.

Installing Thresholds

There are a number of ways to treat the transitions from ceramic tile to other flooring materials. One option is to install a ceramic threshold or saddle (as shown here) that's held in place with thin-set mortar. Thresholds for tile floors (saddles) can be made of marble or a variety of solid-surface materials.

Another possibility for handling transition is to install a wood or metal threshold, as illustrated in the drawing at left. Wood and metal thresholds are easy to install: Just cut them to the correct length and screw or nail them to the subfloor.

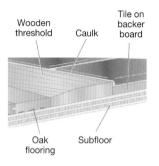

Wooden threshold   Caulk   Tile on backer board

Oak flooring   Subfloor

WOODEN THRESHOLD

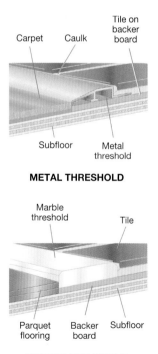

Carpet   Caulk   Tile on backer board

Subfloor   Metal threshold

METAL THRESHOLD

Marble threshold   Tile

Parquet flooring   Backer board   Subfloor

MARBLE THRESHOLD

1 MEASURE AND CUT SADDLE. Since you'll be bonding a saddle to the subfloor with thin-set and the saddle typically fits between a wood frame and trim, you'll need to make some allowance for movement. In general, you want to leave a gap at each end of the saddle equal to the width of the grout joints (these expansion joints will be filled later; see page 119). To determine the length of your saddle, measure from trim to trim (as shown below) and subtract the width of two grout lines. Mark the threshold and cut it to length with a motorized wet saw (see page 92).

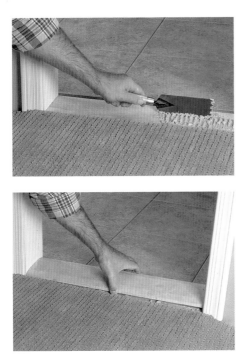

2 **APPLY THE THIN-SET.** Mix up a small amount of thin-set and apply it to the subfloor or underlayment with a notched margin trowel, as shown. Make very sure that this surface is level and that there are no dips or highs, as these will inevitably cause the saddle to crack with use.

3 **SET THE SADDLE.** Now you can set the saddle in the thin-set as shown. Make sure to leave an expansion gap on both sides of the saddle along its length where it meets the flooring, as well as centering it from side to side in the doorway. Allow the thin-set to cure for 48 hours before stepping on the saddle.

4 **FILL THE EXPANSION JOINTS.** When the thin-set has fully cured, go back and fill the expansion joints on the sides and ends of the saddle with 100% silicone, colored to match the grout and/or flooring.

TILE FLOORS

Tile Baseboard

Most flooring tile manufacturers make base trim tiles to match their floor tiles. These typically feature a small cove at the bottom to serve as a smooth transition from wall to floor and to make cleaning easier. But sometimes you may not like how they look, or you simply can't buy trim tiles to match. In cases like this, you can install bullnose tiles like the ones shown here. You can pick a similar color, or a contrasting color as an accent.

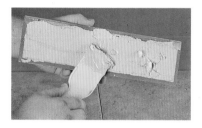

1 BACK-BUTTER THE TILES. Instead of trying to apply thin-set mortar or adhesive to the wall (which is both awkward and difficult to spread at a uniform height), spread the mortar or adhesive on the back of the tile just as you spread butter on a piece of toast—a technique called back-buttering. Keep the adhesive about ¼" away from the top edge to prevent squeeze-out when you press the tile in place.

2 SET THE TILES. Press a trim piece in place and shift it slightly from side to side to help evenly distribute the thin-set.

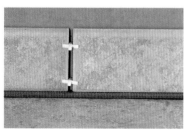

3 ADJUST THE SPACING. Continue adding trim tiles by inserting plastic spacers in between tiles as you work your way down the wall. Allow the thin-set to dry overnight, and remove the spacers.

4 APPLY GROUT. Mix up a small batch of grout and apply it to the gaps between the tiles with a float or a plastic putty knife, as shown. Consider applying a strip of masking tape to the wall above the tile to keep grout off the wall. Use your fingers to press grout into the bullnosed top edge as needed. Scrape off any excess grout with the putty knife, and then switch to a sponge to remove any residue. Let the grout dry, and buff off the haze with a clean, dry cloth.

5 FILL ANY EXPANSION JOINTS. Regardless of the type of base trim you've installed, it's important to seal the gap between the trim and the floor tiles and between the top edge of the trim tiles and the wall. Depending on the type of trim you've installed, this may be grout (for base-trim tiles) or caulk (for bullnose tiles, cove base molding, or wood trim). Sealing the gaps prevents dirt and moisture from working under the tiles and causing damage to either the wall or the floor. Choose a 100% silicone caulk that matches the trim and apply it with a caulk gun as shown.

6

Tile Walls

TILED WALLS ARE GREAT CHOICES for bathrooms and kitchens, of course, but any room can benefit from tile—on a small scale, as well as large. Partial tiling, as well as tiling entire walls, is very popular: You see it in kitchen range murals and wainscoting, to cite just two examples. In this chapter we'll cover ceramic wall tile, tiling a tub surround, tiling a wall with decorative inserts, and installing a range mural.

Ceramic Wall Tile

Tile can bring texture and color to any room. Whether hand-painted or factory-made, mosaic or standard size, tile works with any style. With so many choices in colors, patterns, and sizes, selecting the tile for a wall can be the toughest task. Here's a general design guideline: To keep proper proportions in small spaces like bathrooms or the backsplash in a kitchen, select tiles that are no larger than 4" square. Another good choice is smaller, mosaic tiles (see page 25). Tiles over 4" work better for larger, more open spaces. Spice up your tiled wall with liners and listellos (pages 26–27). A special listello—chair rail—is a favorite trim for many walls.

The general guidelines for tile layout (pages 8–10) apply to walls. There are two additional items to note. First, always use full tiles at the base of a wall, as illustrated in the drawing below. Also, many walls have windows, and it's important that partial tiles around the window be equal on both sides of the window, as shown. Second, unlike on floors, where gravity works for you, gravity tends to work against you when you're tiling a wall. To get around this, temporary battens (page 125) are used to create a level starting point and to support the tile as it's installed. To prepare a wall for tile, you may or may not need to attach backer board and/or a membrane. For a typical wet install, see pages 15 and 133–140.

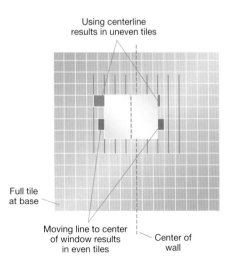

Using centerline results in uneven tiles

Full tile at base

Moving line to center of window results in even tiles

Center of wall

1 INSTALL A BATTEN SECOND ROW UP.

The first step to tiling a wall is to locate where the second row of tile up from the floor begins (see page 62 for more on this). Once you've located this point, install a batten directly under to serve as a starting point for tiling. A 1×2 or smaller scrap of pine is all that's necessary here—just make sure it's straight. Then fasten it to the wall studs as shown, taking care to check it with a level.

2 DRAW THE REFER- ENCE LINES.

With the batten in place, the next step is to lay out the reference lines for your pattern. For the tile shown here we used a running-bond pattern (see page 108) and laid out the lines using a level to make sure they were plumb.

3 APPLY THE THIN-SET. If your tile doesn't extend all the way up to the ceiling, mask off the wall above the area to be tiled to keep it free from adhesive and grout. It's also a good idea to mask off the floor as well. Then, using the rec-ommended-sized notched trowel (see page 46), apply thin-set mortar, working about a 2-foot-square area at a time.

4 INSTALL THE SECOND ROW OF TILES. Now you can start laying the second row of tiles. Since we used ceramic tile with built-in spacer tabs here, we could rest the tiles directly on the batten, as shown. Start at one of the reference lines and fill in the area you've mortared.

PRO TIP

Sealing Exterior Walls

If the wall you'll be tiling is an exterior wall, consider adding a moisture barrier. Even in a well-sealed house, moisture can and does seep through exterior walls in the form of condensation. If left to pass on to the tiled wall, this moisture can break down adhe-sives and create mold and mildew. You can prevent this by installing a layer of 4-mil plastic underneath your underlayment before tiling, as illustrated in the bottom drawing.

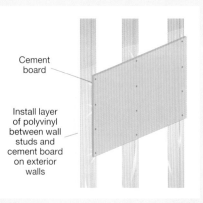

Cement board

Install layer of polyvinyl between wall studs and cement board on exterior walls

5 ESTABLISH THE TILING PATTERN. Once you have the second row in place, you can begin laying tiles above it to establish your tiling pattern. The running-bond pattern shown here works especially well for walls, as it offsets the grout lines and will help hide any variations in tile spacing or grout thickness.

6 CONTINUE IN A PYRAMID SHAPE. Work your way carefully up the wall, adding tiles and applying mortar as necessary. The pyramid method of tiling shown here does a great job of keeping your pattern on track because it lets you make slight adjustments as needed as you move up the wall. If you're planning on installing a liner or listello (as shown here), stop tiling at the specified height of the trim.

7 INSTALL ANY LINERS OR LISTELLOS. Liners and listellos do a great job of breaking up an otherwise boring field of tile by adding visual interest. The only challenge to installing liners and listellos is that most don't come with built-in spacers. So you'll have to use plastic spacers to set the grout line between them and the field tiles. Also, you'll probably find it easier to back-butter (page 85) these narrow trim pieces instead of applying thin-set to the underlayment. For listellos with recesses on their back side, it's usually best to back-butter and apply thin-set to the underlayment.

Box Extenders

Almost any time you tile a wall, you'll encounter a problem with switches and receptacles. The added thickness of the tile and/or backer board makes it tough to reinstall switches and receptacles. What you need is a way to extend the switch or receptacle out so it ends up flush with the tile. The solution? A box extender. Box extenders come in different types and sizes. Some are backless boxes (as shown here); others are plastic tabs that slip between the switch or receptacle and the existing box.

8 CONTINUE ABOVE THE LINERS/LISTELLOS. Once
you've laid a row of liners or listellos (if applicable), apply
more thin-set and continue laying field tiles above the trim pieces,
as shown. When you reach the ceiling (or set height of the wall
tile), install any partial or trim tiles (if applicable).

9 REMOVE THE BATTEN. Odds are that by the time you've
tiled your area to its full height, the thin-set that's holding the
second row of tile in place above the batten is fairly well set. This
means that you can safely remove the batten, as shown. If the
tiles do start to shift, leave the batten in place longer to give the
adhesive more time to set up.

10 INSTALL THE BOTTOM ROW. With the batten removed, you can install the bottom row of tiles. Use the end of your notched trowel (or a smaller notched margin trowel) to apply thin-set to the underlayment under the second row. Then install the bottom row of tiles as shown, taking care to butt them fully up against the second row. It's important here that you leave an appropriate-sized expansion joint between the tile and the existing flooring (for more on expansion joints, see page 16).

11 ADD TAPE TO SUPPORT TILES. To prevent the bottom row of tiles you've just installed from sliding down into the expansion joint, apply strips of masking tape as shown.

12 SET THE TILES.

Whenever you've tiled a 2- to 4-foot-square area, stop and level the tiles. The shop-made caul described on page 89 is perfect for this. Hold the caul so that it's diagonal on the tiles, as shown, and tap it with a hammer or rubber mallet to level the tiles. Continue like this, sliding the caul diagonally over the tiles and striking as you go.

PRO TIP

Story Stick

Although accurate measurements are good, story sticks are better for laying out and checking tile patterns. Why? Because they're made using the actual tile and spacers—and this is more accurate than measuring. To make a story stick, simply lay out your tile pattern and insert spacers as needed. Then transfer the tile, grout line, and trim locations directly onto the stick. Now you can use the stick to check or lay out a pattern in seconds—no measurements required.

TILE WALLS

13 **APPLY THE GROUT.** After you've let the thin-set dry overnight, go back and remove any plastic spacers (if applicable). Then mix up a small batch of grout and apply it to the tile with a grout float. Angle the float to squeegee off the excess, and switch to a damp sponge to remove any residue. Allow the grout to dry to a haze; then buff this off with a clean, dry cloth.

QUICK FIX

Corner Tiles

If your tile continues on to an adjacent wall, check to see whether your tile manufacturer offers corner tiles. These preshaped tiles allow you to wrap around inside and outside corners with ease, instead of having to miter the ends of the tile with a wet saw. You'll find that outside corners (like the one shown here) are much more common than inside corners.

Tiling a Tub Surround

In bathrooms, tiling the surround above a tub is one of the most popular tiling projects. This is especially common in remodel work, where an existing one-piece tub/shower unit has been removed. Unless some walls (and most likely the door into the bathroom) are removed, you can't fit a new one-piece unit into the room since they're designed only for new construction. But you can fit in a new tub. And if you want a shower, you'll need to protect the surrounding walls: Tile is the perfect material for this. Note that you'll need to install a waterproofing membrane (pages 34 and 80–82) over your underlayment to prevent moisture from seeping through and damaging the wall and underlying framing.

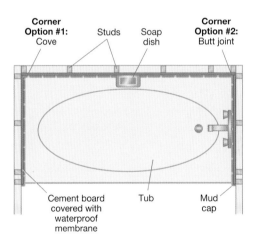

Corner Option #1: Cove   Studs   Soap dish   Corner Option #2: Butt joint

Cement board covered with waterproof membrane   Tub   Mud cap

Also, unless you're tiling the surround from tub to ceiling, you'll need some type of transition from the tile to the wall. Special trim tiles called endcaps or mudcaps are curved on top to compensate for the difference in thickness between the two surfaces—most commonly caused by backer board, as shown in the drawing above.

1 INSTALL DRYWALL IF NECESSARY. If you've removed an old one-piece tub/shower unit, you'll need to install drywall before installing your underlayment and membrane. It's always best to use moisture-resistant drywall (often called greenboard) in bathrooms, due to the high-moisture environment. Note that in some localities, it is permissible to install $\frac{1}{2}$" cement board directly over wall studs to serve as a base for tile.

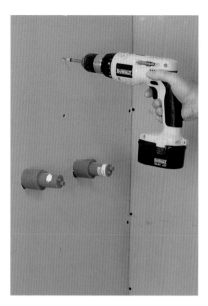

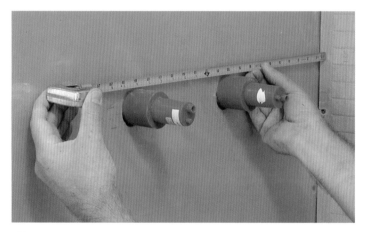

2 LOCATE PLUMBING CUTOUTS. With the drywall installed, you can move on to the backer board. Since one of the end walls has the plumbing for the shower, you'll need to locate and mark any openings required for the plumbing. The number of openings will depend on your tub/shower valve. These can range from one to three. Carefully measure out from one wall and up from the tub, and transfer these measurements to your backer board.

3 CUT PLUMBING OPENINGS. After you've located the cutouts for plumbing and have transferred them onto your backer board, centerpunch these locations for your drill bit. Holes can be drilled in backer board with masonry or glass and tile bits, and diamond hole saws (as shown here). With some valves you'll need to cut out an odd-shaped opening: A saber saw fitted with an abrasive blade or a rotary tool can make quick work of cutting this opening.

4 TEST THE FIT. Before trying to install the backer board, make sure to check the fit once you've cut the openings. Adjust the openings as needed until the backer board slips easily into place.

5 INSTALL THE BACKER
BOARD. To install the backer
board, start by locating and
marking the wall studs with a stud
finder. Next, using the fasteners
recommended by the backer board
manufacturer, attach the board to
the wall studs. When moisture is
present, we always use screws
instead of nails, as they tend to
hold better over time—just make
sure the screws are galvanized.

6 TAPE AND SEAL THE
JOINTS. Any seams in the
backer board need to be taped and sealed. Cover them with fiberglass mesh tape (page 35), as shown in the bottom left photo.
Then apply a layer of thin-set mortar over the tape with a trowel
or putty knife, as shown in the bottom right photo. With the joints
sealed, your next step is to install a waterproofing membrane (see
pages 80–82). We installed 4-mil plastic for our surround.

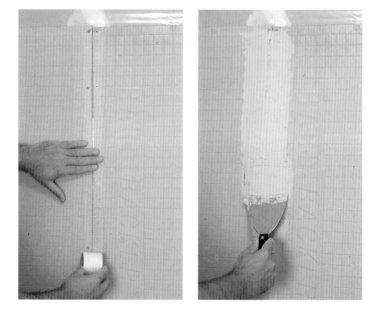

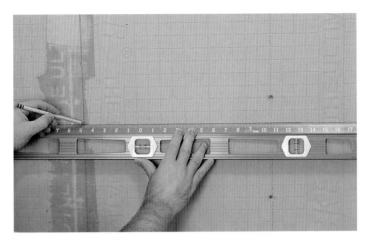

7 MARK THE REFERENCE LINES. Once the membrane is installed, you can mark your reference lines to establish your tile pattern; see page 63 for the recommended layout sequence. Take your time laying this out, and consider making and using a story stick (page 131) to help lay out the tile pattern.

8 APPLY THE THIN-SET. How you approach tiling the surround will depend on a couple of things: how you're treating the corners (whether or not you're using cove trim), and what type of trim tiles you're using around the perimeter of the surround. We opted to tile into the corners, leaving an expansion joint. This allowed us to tile the back wall first, as shown. Use the recommended notched trowel (page 46) to spread adhesive onto your underlayment.

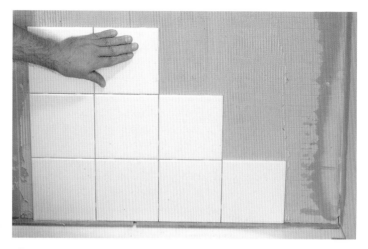

9 INSTALL THE FIELD TILES. Now you can begin installing the field tiles. Since there needs to be an expansion joint between the tile and the tub, you'll need to raise the bottom row of tiles off the tub surface. We used strips of ¼" hardboard for this, as shown. Press the tiles into the adhesive with a slight twisting motion. Stop occasionally and check for proper adhesive coverage (see page 85).

PRO **T**IP

Full Tiles at Trim

Pros always plan their tile patterns so that they'll end up with full field tiles at the corners and around the perimeter of the tub, as shown. This takes careful thought and generally requires tiling from the trim over toward the corner. This way, if partial tiles are needed, they can be installed in the less noticeable corners.

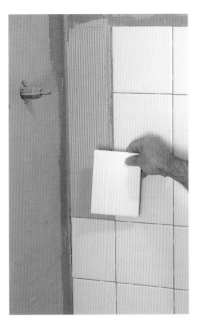

10 INSTALL ANY PARTIAL TILES.

Continue installing as many full tiles as possible, stopping when you reach the height of your liners or listellos (if applicable). Then measure, mark, and cut any partial tiles; see pages 66–67 and 90–94, respectively. Once cut, install the partial tiles, making sure to leave room for expansion joints.

11 INSTALL THE LINERS.

If you are using liners or listellos, now is the time to install them. Note that almost all of these trim pieces do not have built-in spacing tabs, so you'll need to insert plastic spacers between the trim and the field tiles. In many cases, liners and listellos will benefit from back-buttering (page 85) in addition to applying thin-set to the underlayment. The additional adhesive helps ensure a good bond.

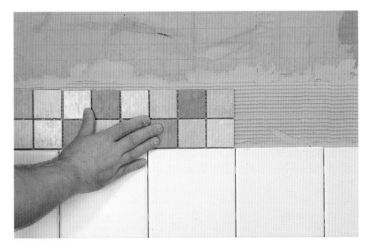

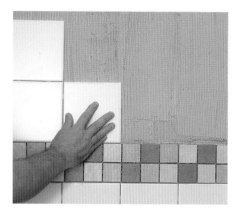

12 CONTINUE TILING ABOVE THE LINERS. With the liners or listellos in place, continue installing full and partial tiles above them until you reach the desired height.

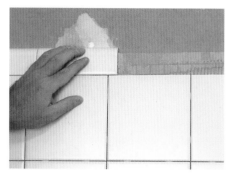

13 INSTALL THE CORNER AND EDGE TRIM. When all your field tiles and partials are in place, go ahead and install any trim pieces like mud-caps (as shown here) or bullnose trim.

14 APPLY THE GROUT. After you've allowed the thin-set to dry overnight, you can fill the gaps between the tiles with grout. Here again, you'll want to work in small areas at a time. Press the grout into the gaps with a grout float; then, holding the float at an angle, squeegee off the excess. Follow this with a damp sponge to remove any excess grout, and let dry. Wipe off the haze with a clean, dry cloth.

Wall Tile with Decorative Inserts

One of the truly great things about tile is that you don't have to be satisfied with the shapes available in stores—you can custom-cut your own shapes. This lets you design personalized patterns using your own shapes—the possibilities are limitless. For example, look at the pattern illustrated in the drawing below. By simply cutting off the corners of tiles at an angle, you can create a space for a decorative insert. Some tile manufacturers offer tile shapes similar to this but only in a few colors, patterns, and textures. We'll show you how to custom-cut your tile on page 143.

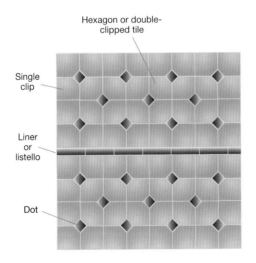

Hexagon or double-clipped tile

Single clip

Liner or listello

Dot

Also, decorative inserts—or "dots" as they're sometimes called—can be quite expensive. To save on costs, consider using individual mosaic tiles cut from a sheet, as we did here. Most mosaic tile is quite reasonably priced, and there's a wide variety of styles, colors, and patterns available.

1 **MARK YOUR REFER-ENCE LINES.** Once you've determined the shape of your custom tiles and the size of your inserts (see the opposite page), your first step is to lay out reference lines on the underlayment as a guide for laying tile. This can be as simple as a plumb vertical line (as shown here), or as complicated as a running-bond pattern (see page 108). If your wall is in a wet area, as here, you'll be marking your reference lines directly on the waterproofing membrane.

2 **APPLY THE THIN-SET.** Mix up enough thin-set to cover a 2- to 4-foot-square area, and apply it to the under-layment with the appropriate-sized notched trowel (see page 46 for recom-mended trowel sizes).

Custom-Cutting Tile

◤◣ Custom-cutting tile is difficult—the tough part is cut-
◥◤ ting identical tiles. But there's a simple way you can
do this: Use a cutting jig. A cutting jig is nothing more than
a scrap of plywood that's notched to hold your tile in a set
position. A tile is inserted in the jig, and the jig rides along
the fence of your tile saw. Just slide the jig and tile together
into the blade and it'll make an exact cut. To make a jig that
creates octagonal tiles (as shown here), see below.

1 MARK THE CUT.
To define how much
material you want to
remove from the corner of
a tile, use your decorative
insert as a template. Place
the insert on the tile so it
spans the adjacent sides

equally, as shown in the photo above. Then add the desired
width for your grout line. Use this to define the notch in your
plywood scrap, and cut the notch in the scrap.

**2 CUT THE TILES WITH
THE JIG.** Position the
fence on your tile saw so
that the jig will just slide past
the blade. Insert a tile in the
jig, turn on the saw, and
make the cut as shown in
the photo at left. Repeat for
any other corners that you're
removing, and do this to your
remaining tiles.

TILE WALLS

3 INSTALL THE FIELD TILES. If you'll be installing cove base, make sure to start your first row of tiles above the baseline for the cove base; see page 62 for more on this. Press each tile into the thin-set with a twisting motion to help distribute the adhesive. If you're using tile without built-in spacers (as shown here), insert plastic spacers between the tiles as you go.

4 INSTALL THE DECORATIVE INSERTS. As you create pockets for the decorative inserts, install the inserts as shown in the photos below and at right. Use plastic spacers if necessary to lock them in place until the adhesive sets up.

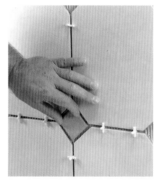

5 CONTINUE TILING. Continue tiling and adding inserts until you achieve the desired height. Cut and install any partial tiles, and install trim tiles as desired. After the adhesive has set up overnight, remove the plastic spacers and apply grout, as described on pages 96–98.

Installing a Range Mural

Kitchen range murals are gaining popularity as tiling projects because they add a lot of flair to an otherwise ho-hum backsplash. Most are installed along with a backsplash (see pages 160–165). Murals can also be installed by themselves, as long as you frame the mural with an appropriate trim tile such as a bullnose. A range mural can be as simple as the framed diagonal tiles illustrated in the drawing above, or as complicated as a highly textured hand-painted scene made up of individual tiles.

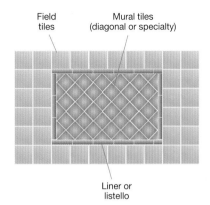

Field tiles

Mural tiles (diagonal or specialty)

Liner or listello

1 INSTALL THE BACKER BOARD. Just as if you were installing a tile backsplash, it's best to set mural tile on some type of backer board. We chose ¼" fiber-based backer board here because it's lighter than cement board and easier to work with. To install backer board for a backsplash or range mural, you'll first need to find and mark the locations of the wall studs. Fasten the backer board to the studs with screws or nails (as shown here) every 6" to 8".

TILE WALLS

2 LOCATE THE CENTERS. In most cases, you'll want your mural centered over the range. So begin the layout by finding and marking the center of the range, as shown in the top photo.

3 LAY OUT THE PATTERN. Use the centerline as the starting point to lay out your mural pattern on the backer board as shown in the bottom left photo. A framing square works great for this, as it allows you to draw perfectly perpendicular lines. Instead of measuring tile, pros will mock up the mural and use this to create the layout; see the sidebar below.

P R O   T I P

Mock Up the Mural

◤◥ Pros know that there can ◣◿ be a lot of variation in tile— especially with tiles for range murals, since these are often handmade. Instead of measuring individual tiles and calculating the size of the mural, a pro will dry-assemble the mural, as shown in the photo below. Then they'll measure it and use these measurements to lay out the mural on the backer board.

4 **INSTALL THE STARTING BATTEN.** Since murals are typically raised above the range and the surrounding area is filled in with backsplash field tiles, you'll want to install a batten to support the mural tiles. Cut a scrap of wood to length and temporarily attach it to the wall studs, as shown in the photo above.

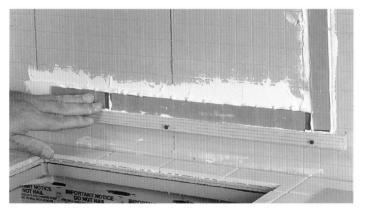

5 **INSTALL THE LINERS.** There are two ways you can install the mural: liners first or field tiles first. Either way is fine, as long as you've mocked up the mural (page 146) and have laid it out accurately on the backer board. We chose to install the liner tiles first, as shown in the bottom photo. If you're not confident about your pattern, you may find it better to install the field tiles first, then wrap the liners around them.

6 APPLY THE THIN-SET.

Depending on the size of the mural, you may or may not be able to apply thin-set to the entire mural area. Note that since we used glass mosaic tile as the liner, we used white adhesive (for more on working with glass tile, see Chapter 8). Apply the adhesive with the recommended-sized notched trowel (see page 46).

7 INSTALL THE FIELD TILES.

With the liners in place, go ahead and begin installing the field tiles of the mural, as shown in the bottom photo. Start at the bottom and work your way up. If your mock-up and layout were accurate, the tiles should fit perfectly. If not, you should still have plenty of time to shift tiles as needed before the adhesive sets up.

8 INSTALL THE SURROUNDING FIELD TILES. Allow the mural adhesive to set up overnight before removing the bottom batten. Now you can surround the mural with the backsplash field tiles as shown in the top photo, cutting partial tiles as needed.

9 APPLY THE GROUT. Let the adhesive set up overnight and then remove any spacers used. Then mix up a small batch of grout and apply it to the tile with a grout float. Angle the float to squeegee off the excess, and switch to a sponge to remove any residue. Allow the grout to dry to a haze and then buff this off with a clean, dry cloth.

TILE WALLS

7

Tile Countertops

COUNTERTOPS LOVE TILE, and so do homeowners: It's durable, inexpensive, readily available, and easy to install. Sure, it's messier and more time-consuming than other countertop installations, but if you take it one step at a time, each task is simple and easy—even if you've never laid tile before. In this chapter, we'll show you how to tile a countertop, a back-splash, a kitchen island, and a bathroom sink top.

Tiled Countertop

There are really only two types of countertops that you can install yourself: tile, and post-formed plastic laminate tops. The problem with post-formed tops is that they're available only in limited sizes, colors, and patterns. With tile, there are no such limitations. You can make the countertop any size you want and use any tile that strikes your fancy. With tile you also have many choices for edging and backsplashes (see pages 157 and 158, respectively.)

There is one potential drawback to a tile countertop: the grout lines. If left unsealed, grout is easily stained by food spills. But this can be avoided by applying grout sealer (page 98). The secret to grout longevity is to reapply the sealer regularly; see the manufacturer's instructions on how often this should be done. With the proper preparation, you can cover just about any surface with tile. Tiling over existing plastic laminate is possible, as long as the laminate is securely bonded to the countertop. But in most cases, you'll be installing backer board as a foundation for the tile, as illustrated in the drawing below.

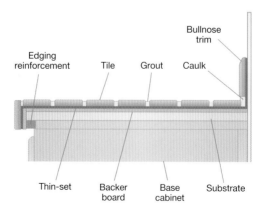

Bullnose trim

Edging reinforcement   Tile   Grout   Caulk

Thin-set   Backer board   Base cabinet   Substrate

1 INSTALL A BACKER BOARD. Quarter-inch fiber-based backer board makes an excellent foundation for tile. To attach it to the countertop, first apply a layer of thin-set using a ⅛"×⅛" V-notch trowel. Cut the backer board to fit as needed and secure it with the appropriate fastener. We used a narrow-crown stapler loaded with galvanized staples. This is an excellent way to quickly secure backer board.

2 ADD BACKER BOARD TO THE EDGE. Since you'll also be applying tile to the front edge of the countertop, you'll want to install strips of backer board along the front edge. Here again, apply thin-set first and then cut and secure the strips to the counter edge with appropriate fasteners.

TILE COUNTERTOPS

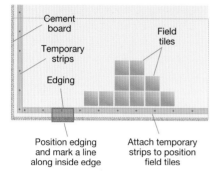

Cement board

Temporary strips

Edging

Field tiles

Position edging and mark a line along inside edge

Attach temporary strips to position field tiles

TOP VIEW

3 INSTALL THE BATTENS. Whether you're using counter edging or bullnose edging (as we did here), the next step is to locate and install battens to position the edging tile, as illustrated in the drawing at left. With either edging, mark a line along the edge of the countertop to allow for the width of the tiles. Then align the batten with this line and temporarily attach it to the countertop with nails. (Leave the heads of the nails proud so they'll be easy to remove later.)

4 APPLY ADHESIVE TO FRONT EDGE. Once you have the batten installed on your underlayment, go ahead and apply thin-set to the area in front of the battens with the appropriate-sized trowel (see page 46). Apply only as much as you can safely tile before the adhesive dries. A notched margin trowel (page 47), with its narrow blade, also works well for this.

5 INSTALL THE BULLNOSE TILES. Now you can install the edging. In our case, we used a two-piece edging comprised of a full-width bullnose tile on top and a narrower bullnose tile under this to create an edging with no grout line on the top front edge. Press the tiles firmly into the adhesive so they butt up against each other (or against the plastic spacers, if applicable).

6 **INSTALL THE FRONT EDGING.** If you're using a two-piece edging (as we did), go ahead and install the front trim piece. Since this piece is narrower than the full-width bullnose tiles on top, it's easier to back-butter the tiles (page 85) than it is to apply adhesive to the narrow strips of backer board attached to the edge of the countertop.

7 **APPLY ADHESIVE TO THE FIELD.** With the edging in place, remove the temporary battens and apply adhesive to the area where you'll be installing full field tiles (middle photo). Work an area roughly 2 feet square.

Seal Countertop Edges

◤◥ Most countertops use an engineered panel for the substrate, such as particleboard, plywood, or MDF (medium-density fiber-board). Although each of these is flat and provides an excellent foundation for backer board, they do all have a problem with moisture. Unprotected edges will soak up water like a sponge. That's why pros seal the edges of the opening with a couple of coats of latex paint or carpenter's glue (as shown here). This is added insurance that if the seal under the sink fails, the countertop won't be damaged.

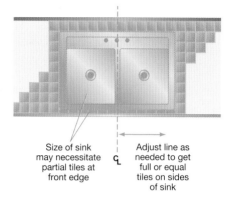

Size of sink may necessitate partial tiles at front edge

C_L

Adjust line as needed to get full or equal tiles on sides of sink

TILES AT AND AROUND THE SINK. The most complicated part of tiling a countertop is tiling around a sink. The tricky part is positioning the tiles so you end up with evenly spaced tiles on both sides of the opening. Here's how to handle this: Begin by placing a row of tiles along the front edge of the sink. Then measure the tiles at each end to the center of the opening. Adjust the tiles as necessary (as shown above) until the excess on each end is the same. Then mark the end of the tiles and use a framing square to extend this line to the backsplash. This line is the starting point for the entire countertop.

8 SET THE FIELD TILES. Begin placing full field tiles at your start mark and press them firmly into the adhesive, using a slight twisting motion to better spread the adhesive. Make sure to leave an expan-  sion joint where the tile meets the back wall and any side walls (for more on expansion joints for countertops, see page 17).

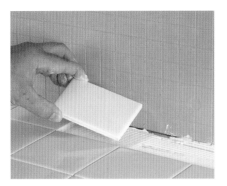

9 INSTALL ANY PARTIALS. Once all of the field tiles in this area are installed, mark, cut, and install any partial tiles. See pages 66–67 for marking partial tiles and pages 90–94 for information on cutting tiles.

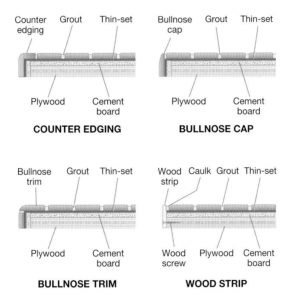

Counter edging | Grout | Thin-set

Plywood | Cement board

COUNTER EDGING

Bullnose cap | Grout | Thin-set

Plywood | Cement board

BULLNOSE CAP

Bullnose trim | Grout | Thin-set

Plywood | Cement board

BULLNOSE TRIM

Wood strip | Caulk | Grout | Thin-set

Wood screw | Plywood | Cement board

WOOD STRIP

EDGING OPTIONS. The drawing above illustrates four common edging treatments: counter edging, bullnose cap, bullnose trim, and wood edging. The wood strip is the simplest to install but tends to show wear over time. The next easiest is counter edging, as it is just one piece. Bullnose cap and bullnose trim aren't much more difficult to install—it's just that there are two pieces to install instead of one.

10 APPLY THE GROUT.

APPLY THE GROUT. With all the edging, field, and partial tiles installed, once the adhesive has dried overnight you can apply grout. First, go back and remove any plastic spacers (if used). Then mix up a small batch of grout and apply it to the tile with a grout float. Angle the float to squeegee off the excess and switch to a sponge to remove any residue. Allow the grout to dry to a haze and then buff this off with a clean, dry cloth.

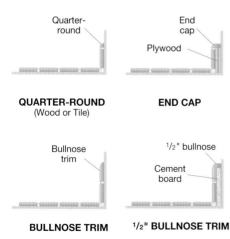

Quarter-round

QUARTER-ROUND
(Wood or Tile)

Bullnose trim

BULLNOSE TRIM

End cap

Plywood

END CAP

$^1/_2$" bullnose

Cement board

$^1/_2$" **BULLNOSE TRIM**

BACKSPLASH OPTIONS. Backsplash options for a tiled countertop include: quarter-round (wood or tile), end cap, and bullnose trim. Each of these is easy to install (see page 164 for yet another option). Additionally, you may choose to tile the entire wall area behind the countertop (pages 160–165) or install a range mural (pages 145–149).

11 **CAULK THE EXPANSION JOINTS.** All that's left is to fill in any expansion joints with 100% color-matched silicone and reinstall any fixtures. See below for a quick way to reinstall a sink.

Flexible Supply Lines

The quickest way to hook up the supply lines on a sink is to use flexible supply lines. These lines run between shutoff valves and fixtures—usually in tight, cramped spaces. Any flexibility in these situations is a big

plus. Flexible supply lines are available with two different types of outer protection: braided metal and vinyl mesh. They come in a variety of pre-set lengths, complete with captive connecting nuts. When buying flexible supply lines, you're better off long than short; any excess can bend to one side. If they're way too long, you can even loop them.

TILE COUNTERTOPS

Tiling a Backsplash

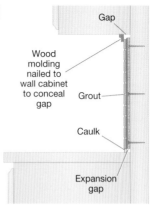

Gap

Wood molding nailed to wall cabinet to conceal gap

Grout

Caulk

Expansion gap

Tile is one of the best all-around, low-maintenance surfaces for a kitchen. No wonder it's the number one choice for protecting the walls behind a countertop. This area, appropriately named the "backsplash," takes a lot of punishment. But a tile backsplash can handle the day-to-day splattering: It's virtually immune to water and food spills, and can also take hard knocks from countertop appliances being pushed around.

A full-tile backsplash (like the one illustrated in the drawing above) is a great way to add color and texture to your kitchen. Colorful mosaic tiles, hand-painted tiles, and glossy tiles can all make a statement. You can also dress up a full-tile backsplash with a range mural (see pages 145–149). Alternatively, a partial tile backsplash will protect a wall, and it installs quickly; see pages 158 and 164–165 for partial backsplash options.

1 ATTACH BACKER BOARD. The type of wall covering behind your countertop will determine whether or not you need to attach backer board. Some older homes have plastic laminate on the wall, and all you need do here is rough up the laminate with coarse sandpaper before applying thin-set mortar. If instead the wall is covered with drywall, it's best to attach backer board to prevent moisture in the thin-set from seeping in and damaging the wall.

2 **TEST THE PATTERN.** If you're planning on a decorative pattern for your backsplash—such as a group of contrast-colored tiles (as shown here)—it's a good idea to lay out the actual tiles to test the pattern in advance to make sure it'll work.

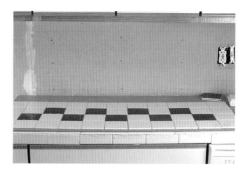

3 **MASK OFF THE WALL AND COUNTERTOP AREA.** With the backer board in place, mask off the wall area and cabinets above the backsplash to keep thin-set and grout off these surfaces; then mask off the countertop as well.

4 **MARK ANY REFERENCE LINES.** Even if you're planning on using decorative tiles, you'll still want to locate and mark reference lines on the backer board. At minimum you'll want a starting point that will ensure equal partial tiles at both ends of the backsplash.

5 **APPLY THE ADHESIVE.** After marking your reference lines on the backer board, mix up enough thin-set to work a 2- to 4-square foot area and apply it to the backer board with the appropriate-sized notched trowel (see page 46 for recommended sizes). Alternatively, pre-mixed organic mastics work great for wall tile, as they offer excellent "grab" characteristics. This helps keep tile from sliding out of position due to gravity.

6 **SET THE FIRST ROW.** The next step is to set the full tiles. Start at the bottom at your marked starting point and work your way up, pressing tiles in place with a slight twisting motion to help distribute the adhesive. See the sidebar on page 163 for an easy way to set the expansion joint between the backsplash and the counter-

top. If necessary, insert plastic spacers between the tiles to create even gaps. Most ceramic wall tiles (like the ones shown here) have built-in tabs on the tiles for spacing.

7 CONTINUE TILING. Specialty tiles are available that can add visual interest to your backsplash. Alternatively, you can simply use contrast-color tiles (as shown here). Continue adding field tiles and then mark, cut, and install any partial tiles as needed. See pages 66–67 for marking partial tiles and pages 90–94 for information on cutting tiles. After you've applied grout and it's dry, remember to run a bead of silicone between the tile and countertop to create a seal.

See pages 66–67 for marking partial tiles and pages 90–94 for information on cutting tiles.

P R O   T I P

Setting Gaps for Expansion Joints

◥◣ An expansion joint is called for where the tiled back-
◣◥ splash meets the countertop. This gap allows the different materials of the countertop and adjacent wall to move independently as the humidity changes, without damaging the tile. An easy way to create the gap for the expansion joint is to lay a ¼" hardboard spacer flat on the countertop before installing the tile. Once the tile adhesive has set, slide out the spacer and fill the gap with 100% silicone colored to match the countertop or tile.

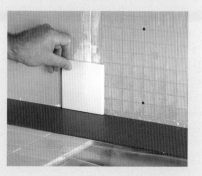

TILE COUNTERTOPS

Bullnose Backsplash

◤◥ While you can install a partial tile backsplash directly onto drywall (see page 158), there's a stur-
dier option that guarantees that moisture won't penetrate into the walls and underlying framing. It's a bullnose backsplash, as illustrated in the top right drawing. The foun-

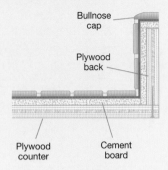

Bullnose cap

Plywood back

Plywood counter

Cement board

dation of this backsplash is a layer of plywood that's screwed to the back edge of the countertop, as shown. Then the plywood is wrapped with backer board and the tile is installed. This creates a virtually watertight backsplash. Alternatively, if you don't want to lose the counter space taken up by the added thickness of the plywood, you can attach a strip of backer board to the wall and cap it with wood or tile quarter-round, as shown on page 158.

1 ATTACH THE BACKER BOARD.
Start by cutting a plywood strip to width and length. The width of the strip is determined by the height of the tile or tiles you'll be using, plus the width of the grout lines. The best way to determine width is to lay out the tile (with spacers if applicable) and measure across the tiles. Then cut strips of backer board and attach it to the plywood with appropriate fasteners. Note that we cut our backer board $1/4$" narrower than the plywood to allow for the backer board on the countertop to slide under it.

2 **SET THE FIELD TILES.** You have two options for installing the backsplash. You can attach it to the counter-top now and then tile, or tile it and attach it to the countertop later (as shown here). As long as

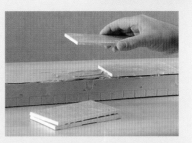

the back wall is plumb, you can install it after it's tiled; but if the back wall is out of plumb or wavy, it's best to attach first and then tile. Mix up enough thin-set for the job, and apply it to the backer board with the appropriate-sized trowel (see page 46). You'll find that the narrow blade of a notched margin trowel (page 47) works well in this narrow space. Then install the field tiles by pressing them into the adhesive with a slight twisting motion to help spread the adhesive.

3 **APPLY THE BULLNOSE TRIM.** When you have all the field tiles in place, attach the bullnose trim on top. We used a complementary color tile to add visual interest. You can either apply adhesive to the top of the bullnose or back-butter the tile (page 85). Allow the adhesive to dry overnight and then apply grout, as described on pages 96–98.

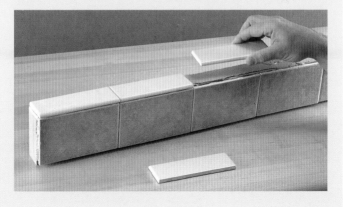

TILE COUNTERTOPS

Tiling a Kitchen Island

Tiling a kitchen island is similar to tiling a countertop, with one big difference: The edge tile wraps all the way around an island top. To prevent unattractive partials tiles, you'll need to do some advance planning. The best way to prevent partial tiles is to design the size of the top around the tiles you're using. To do this, lay out the tile in the desired pattern—using full tiles only, along with your edging trim—then measure and cut your kitchen island countertop to these dimensions, as illustrated in the drawing above. If you have an existing island top and you can't alter its size, try working with different-sized tiles to create a pattern that uses only full tiles. Mixing and matching tile widths is a good way to make this work; try a set of narrow liners down the middle of the island or as a frame for the field tiles.

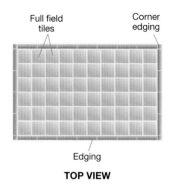

Full field tiles

Corner edging

Edging

TOP VIEW

1 INSTALL THE BACKER BOARD. Cut backer board to size and also cut strips to attach to the edge of the countertop. Attach the backer board and edge strips with galvanized screws or nails (bottom photos).

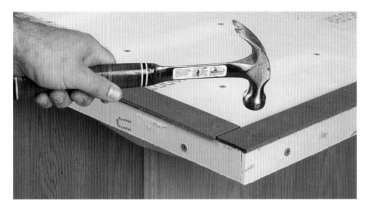

2 **INSTALL TEMPORARY BATTENS.** If you plan to edge the countertop with counter edging, as shown here, the next step is to temporarily attach strips of wood to the countertop to serve as guides for the tiles. Mark a line along the edge of the counter-top to allow for the width of the counter edging. Then align the batten with this line and temporarily attach it to the countertop with nails. For wood edging where the tiles will be flush with the front edge of the countertop, temporarily attach a strip of wood to the front edge of the countertop to serve as a guide.

3 **APPLY THE ADHESIVE.** Mix up a batch of thin-set and apply it to the backer board with the appropriate-sized notched trowel (see page 46), working in a 2- to 4-foot-square area.

4 SET THE FIELD TILES. Begin laying tiles by working out from the corner. The tiles shown here have built-in tabs for spacing; other tiles may require plastic spacers to set the gaps between the tiles. Press a tile firmly into the thin-set, wiggling it slightly as you press down to spread the adhesive.

5 INSTALL ANY PARTIALS. If for some reason you couldn't get a full tile pattern to work out, go back and mark, cut, and install any partial tiles. See pages 66–67 for marking partial tiles and pages 90–94 for information on cutting tiles. After placing the tiles, you can set them. Setting tiles presses them firmly into the mortar and also levels the surface. A simple way to do this is to place a 1-foot square of ³⁄₄"-thick plywood on the tile and give it a few raps with a rubber mallet.

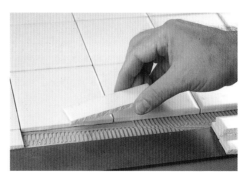

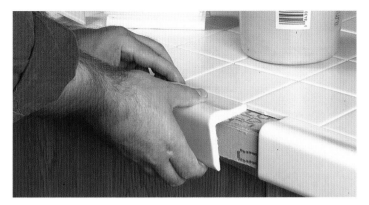

6 **INSTALL THE EDGE TRIM.** When all the tiles have been set, you can turn your attention to the edging tiles. Start by removing the temporary battens. Then apply thin-set to the tiles. This is less messy than applying it to the backer board. Just slather some adhesive on both back inside faces of the tile and press the tile in place.

7 **APPLY THE GROUT.** Let the thin-set dry overnight and then mix up enough grout to fill in the gaps between the tiles. Apply the grout with a grout float diagonally to the surface to force the grout between the tiles. To remove the excess, hold the float at about a 45-degree angle and scrape the surface, taking care not to pull the grout out from between the tiles. Clean off any residue with a damp sponge. Allow the grout to dry, and buff off the haze with a clean, dry cloth.

A Bathroom Sink Top

What bathroom isn't perfect for ceramic tile? Tile can turn a bath from "blah" to "beautiful," thanks to the enormous choices in textures, colors, patterns, shapes, and sizes. What's especially nice about tiling a bathroom sink top is that the area usually is small, so you can splurge on more expensive tile, like the tumbled marble we used for our sink top. For this project you'll need to choose a sink that's self-rimming—that is, a sink that has a lip that both supports the sink in the opening and also provides the means for a seal between the sink and the tiled countertop, as illustrated in the drawing at left.

Wall can be left bare or backsplash can be added

Silicone under rim creates seal   Cement board   Counter-top   Field tile

Caulk

Sink

Tailpiece   Overflow passage   End cap

1 ADD THICKNESS AROUND EDGES. To make your own custom sink top, start by cutting a piece of ³⁄₄"-thick plywood to size. See the sink's mounting instructions for recommended size and for the size of the opening. Just make sure to size the top large enough to provide extra room under its front and side edges. This will let you add strips of plywood to provide additional thickness to support the edging tile, as shown in the photo at right and illustrated in the drawing above. (Note: See the sidebar on page 173 for information on sizing the edging.)

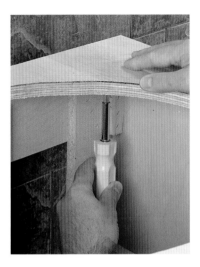

2 ATTACH THE TOP.
Now you can attach the plywood top to your sink base (photo at left). There are a couple of options here. Many bases have brackets installed on the top corner edges of the cabinet. These have mounting holes so that you can thread a screw up through the bracket and into the plywood top (as shown here). Just make sure to size the screw so that it doesn't poke up through the surface of the plywood top. If your sink base doesn't have brackets, apply a bead of silicone caulk around the top perimeter edges and place the top on the base, centering it from side to side. Let the silicone set up overnight before proceeding.

3 TEST-FIT THE SINK.
Before you install backer board, it's a good idea to check the fit of the sink in the top by placing it in the opening, as shown in the bottom photo. If necessary, adjust the opening so the sink fits.

4 **CUT THE BACKER BOARD TO SIZE.** The next step is to cut and attach the backer board. Start by cutting the backer board to fit on the top so its edges are flush with the plywood. Then set the backer board on the top, and from underneath draw the opening onto the bottom of the backer board, as illustrated in the drawing below. Then drill an access hole and cut out the opening, using a saber saw fitted with an abrasive blade (see page 44).

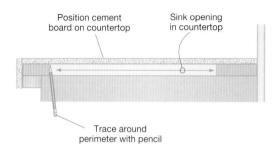

Position cement board on countertop

Sink opening in countertop

Trace around perimeter with pencil

5 **ATTACH BACKER BOARD TO TOP.** To attach backer board to the plywood sink top, first apply a layer of thin-set using a $1/8$"×$1/8$" V-notch trowel. Position the backer board and secure it with appropriate fasteners. We used a narrow-crown stapler, loaded with galvanized staples, for this.

6 **ADD BACKER BOARD EDGING.** Since you'll also be applying tile to the front and side edges of the sink top, you'll want to install strips of backer board along these edges. Here again, apply thin-set first and then cut and secure the strips to the sink top with appropriate fasteners.

Edging and Drawer Clearance

Edging must be narrow so it doesn't interfere with drawer opening

Drawer

TILED COUNTERTOP

Plenty of clearance

Drawer

STANDARD POST-FORMED COUNTERTOP

◥◣ Whenever you add thickness to the perimeter edge of a sink top or countertop to support tile edging, you need to take into account the clearance needed to open and close drawers and cabinets. On a standard post-formed plastic laminate countertop, this isn't an issue: The rolled front edging is small and provides plenty of clearance (bottom drawing). But when you add strips to an existing top, this can be a problem. You'll need to either size the strips to provide clearance or raise the sink top or countertop by inserting shims between the top and the sink base.

TILE COUNTERTOPS

7 APPLY THE ADHE-
SIVE. Mix up a batch
of thin-set and apply it to
the backer board with the
appropriate-sized notched
trowel (see page 46),
working in a small area.
Start in the corner and work
out toward the center of the
sink top. Take care not to
overwork the thin-set, as
this tends to make it dry
quickly and set up before
the tile can be placed.

8 INSTALL THE FIELD
TILES. Begin laying
field tiles by working out
from the corner. The mosaic
tile shown here came in
sheets, so the only spacing
issue was from sheet to
sheet. Individual tiles may
require plastic spacers to
set the gaps between the
tiles. Once all the full tiles
are in place, go back and
mark, cut, and install the
partial tiles. See pages
66–67 for marking partial
tiles and pages 90–94 for
information on cutting tiles.
Note that it's always a good idea to cut partial tiles in advance:
They can be time-consuming to cut, and the thin-set can dry
while you're cutting tile.

9 **INSTALL THE EDGING.** When all the full and partial tiles have been laid, you can install the edging tiles. We used a larger, matching tumbled stone for this, which came in sheets. So all we had to do was cut strips from the sheets. Apply thin-set to  the backer board edging strips with a notched margin trowel. Then press the tile into the adhesive. Use strips of masking tape as shown to prevent the edging from sagging. Allow the thin-set to dry overnight before grouting (see pages 96–98). Note: If you're using tumbled stone, make sure to seal the stone as described below before grouting.

Sealing Stone

■■ Tumbled stone—and many other natural stones—tend to be quite porous. If you don't seal the stone before grouting, the grout will seep into the pores of the stone and discolor it. This can be prevented by first sealing the tile. Stone sealers (photo at left) are available wherever tile is sold. To let the grout bond well to the sides of the tile, it's important that you don't seal the sides of the tile. So don't spray on the sealer. Instead, brush it on as shown. A foam brush works best for this. Immerse the brush in the sealer and wring it out so it's just damp. Then brush it on the tops of the tile. Allow it to dry and then brush on another coat.

TILE COUNTERTOPS

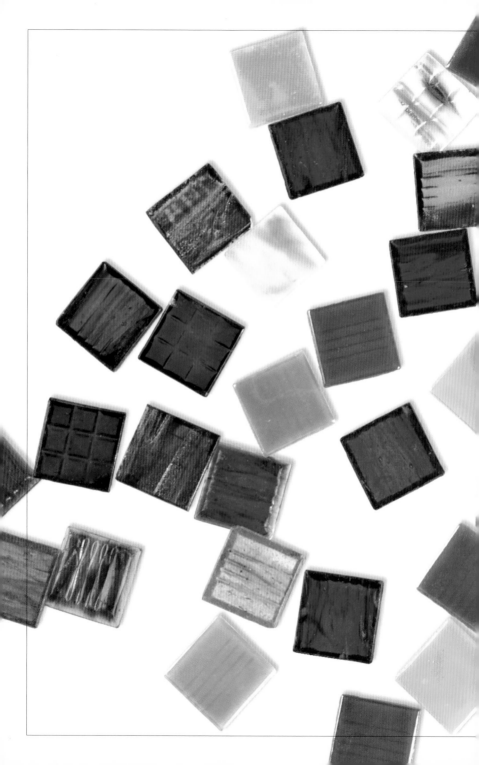

8

Glass Tile

GLASS TILE IS JUST PLAIN GORGEOUS. It sparkles and shimmers like gemstones, and its iridescent rainbow hues look like nothing else in the tile world. Add in its enormous design potential, and you have an upscale material that's gaining popularity fast. Although the techniques of working with glass tile are similar to those for other tile, there are some special rules. In this chapter we'll show you how to work with both mosaic and large glass tile.

Substrates for Glass Tile

Two things determine how durable a beautiful glass tile surface will be: the stability of the underlying substrate, and how well the tile is bonded to this substrate. The following general recommendations are from the Tile Council of North America (TCNA) Handbook for Ceramic Tile Installation (www.tileusa.com). Check with the manufacturer of the glass tile you're using for specific guidelines.

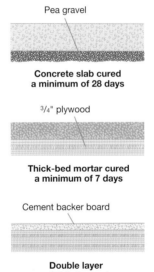

Pea gravel

**Concrete slab cured
a minimum of 28 days**

³/₄" plywood

**Thick-bed mortar cured
a minimum of 7 days**

Cement backer board

**Double layer
of ¹/₂" plywood**

FLOORS. A suitable exterior substrate for a glass tile floor is a concrete slab that has cured for a minimum of 28 days. Acceptable interior substrates include cement mortar beds that have cured at least 7 days (with or without an isolation membrane, depending on the condition of the bed), and cement mortar or cementious backer board, as illustrated in the drawing above.

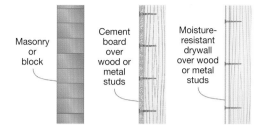

Masonry or block — Cement board over wood or metal studs — Moisture-resistant drywall over wood or metal studs

WALLS. Substrates that work well for glass tile wall installations include: cured masonry or concrete, wood or metal studs covered with a cementious backer board, and wood or metal studs covered with moisture-resistant drywall (greenboard) in dry areas only, as illustrated in the drawing above. In wet installs like showers and bathtub surrounds, the cementious backer board should be covered with a suitable waterproofing membrane (page 34).

UNACCEPTABLE SUBSTRATES

There are a number of substrates that are not suitable for glass tile, as illustrated in the drawing at right. These include: a single-float mortar bed that doesn't have multiple cured scratch coats; a reinforced mortar bed that uses wire reinforcing rated at less than 2.5 pounds per square foot; and wood products such as plywood and lauan, plus engineered wood products like particleboard and MDF (medium-density fiberboard). Wood products generally have too much flexibility, which can result in adhesive bond failure over time.

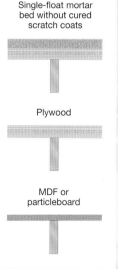

Single-float mortar bed without cured scratch coats

Plywood

MDF or particleboard

GLASS TILE

Adhesives for Glass Tile

Because glass tile is translucent, the color of the bonding material will have a major effect on the outcome of the project. To prevent the adhesive from discoloring the tile, you should always use a white adhesive. Also, because glass tile isn't porous like other tiles, many adhesives are unsuitable for glass tile. Check with the manufacturer of the glass tile you're using for their recommended adhesives—most provide a specific list of brands/products that work with their tile.

MODIFIED THIN-SET MORTAR. You'll find that most glass tile makers recommend one of the many modified latex thin-set mortars. Some require an add-mix; others don't. It's especially important to mix powered adhesives carefully and at generally lower speeds than other thin-sets to prevent bubbles, which can be trapped under the tile— and which will be visible. You should also allow the thin-set to slake at least 15 minutes to let air bubbles trapped within the mix work their way out.

INCORRECT ADHESIVES

There are two adhesives that you should not use to bond glass tile: organic mastics and epoxy. Organic mastics have lower bond strengths than thin-set and they tend to yellow over time, which will discolor the tile. Epoxy has low flexibility and can degrade when exposed to sunlight.

Grout for Glass Tile

As with the adhesive used for glass tile, the grout should also be white to keep from discoloring the tile. Because glass tile isn't porous, the amount of time it takes grout to set up and dry is usually much longer than for other tile materials. Also, as with adhesives, most glass tile manufacturers provide a specific list of approved grout products for use with their tile.

POLYBLEND GROUT. You'll find that many glass tile makers recommend a polyblend sanded or unsanded grout. These can be mixed with water or an add-mix to improve flexibility while enhancing the freeze/thaw characteristics of the grout. Excess grout should initially be removed with clean, dry cheesecloth: This will wick away excess moisture from the grout lines and yet avoid washing out the grout joint. Then a sponge can be used to remove any residue.

UNACCEPTABLE GROUT

Since epoxy grout has low flexibility compared to other grout products and will degrade when exposed to sunlight, most manufacturers do not recommend using it with their glass tile.

Cutting and Shaping Glass Tile

Cutting glass tile is very similar to cutting other tile. Much of the technique is the same (see pages 90–93). The only differences concern the cutting tools (see below and the opposite page).

CONTINUOUS-RIM DIAMOND BLADE. You can cut large glass tile with a motorized wet saw, just as you'd cut other tile. The big difference has to do with the blade. You want to make sure you use a blade with a continuous rim (foreground in the middle photo), instead of a segmented blade like the one mounted in the wet saw. Segmented blades tend to chip the glass surface; continuous blades don't. You can use any standard tile-cutting blade

with a continuous rim, but you'll get better results with blades designed especially for cutting glass. These blades are thinner than standard blades and use less diamond compound, which results in smoother cuts.

CUTTING WITH A WET SAW. Cutting glass tile with a wet saw is just like cutting any other hard tile material. The only difference in technique is that you should feed the tile into the blade slower than you would other materials, since the glass is so hard.

SMOOTH-CUT EDGES

The edges of cut glass tile can be very sharp. To prevent a serious cut to the skin, make sure to smooth any cut tile edges with a rubbing stone, as described on page 45.

SCORING TILE. Smaller glass tiles (like the mosaic tile shown here) can be cut in two ways: You can score a line and snap the tile, or you can nibble the tile. Both operations can be accomplished with a single specialty tool called a glass rod lopper (top photo). These can be found wherever stained-glass supplies are sold. Although designed to cut or "lop off" sections of small-diameter glass rod, they work particularly well with glass tile. Instead of two sharpened jaws like a standard tile

nipper, a glass rod lopper sports a pair of carbide wheels. To score and snap a tile, just close the wheels on the tile and drag it across the surface. Then compress the handles more, and the tile will snap where it was scored.

NIPPING TILE. The glass rod lopper also works great as a nipper. Just insert the tile between the cutting wheels and squeeze the handle, as shown in the bottom photo. As with a tile nipper, you'll have better success and end up with fewer ruined tiles if you take small bites instead of large ones.

GLASS TILE

One-Step Mosaic Tiles

When it comes to installation, glass mosaic tile is very different from other mosaic tile. The major issues are how the tiles are mounted to the sheets and how you apply the adhesive. Some glass tile is mounted to a mesh backing like most mosaic tile, and is installed similarly (with the exception of the adhesive application; see pages 187–189). But other glass mosaic tile comes mounted to a paper backing, like those shown here from Hakatai (www.hakatai.com). Basically, the individual tiles are glued to the backing—no mesh is used. This allows for a unique one-step application technique, as described on the following pages.

1 APPLY THE ADHESIVE. To install paper-backed mosaic tile, start by applying adhesive to the underlayment, using the recommended-sized notched trowel (see page 46).

2 SMOOTH THE ADHESIVE. Next, to prevent the ridges of adhesive from showing through the tile, go back and smooth out the ridges with the flat portion of the trowel, taking care to keep the adhesive uniform in thickness.

3 POSITION THE SHEETS. With the adhesive smoothed, go ahead and position a tile on the adhesive, taking care to adjust the spacing between sheets to match the spacing between the tiles.

4 SET THE TILE. Now go back and press the individual tiles fully into the adhesive. As you do this, excess adhesive will be forced up between the tiles until it hits the paper backing. In effect you're setting the tile and grouting at the same time. Switch to a grout float and press down on the sheets to level the tiles.

5 WET THE PAPER BACKING. Allow the adhesive/grout to sit until it's firm. Then wet the paper backing with a sprayer or sponge. This can take a while to get the paper fully soaked.

6 STRIP OFF THE PAPER BACKING. If you wet the backing sufficiently, it should just peel right off, as shown. Be gentle here so you don't disturb the tiles.

GLASS TILE

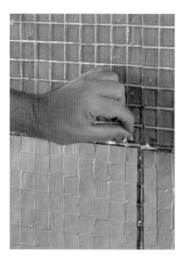

7 **PEEL OFF ANY RESIDUE.** Odds are that you'll find chunks of paper backing stuck to various tiles. Don't apply more water here, as you'll wash out the grout joint. Instead, peel it off with your fingers.

8 **SPONGE THE TILE CLEAN.** Now you can switch to a sponge that's just barely damp to wipe off any residue of paper backing adhesive, and any excess grout. Clean, dry cheesecloth also works well for this. Let the grout dry fully, buff off any haze, and apply a sealer according to the manufacturer's directions.

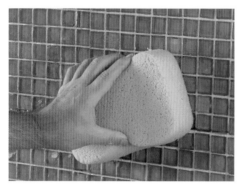

INSUFFICIENT ADHESIVE. Adhesive thickness is critical for the one-step method. Too little grout will not fully support the tiles and can also allow the underlayment to show through. Note that on

some of the lower tiles in the bottom photo, the tiles are discolored by the underlying greenboard.

Two-Step Mosaic Tiles

U nlike one-step mosaic tiles (pages 184–186), two-step mosaic tiles have a standard mesh backing and are installed similarly to other sheet mosaic tile.

1 APPLY THE ADHESIVE. Once you've laid out any reference lines for your tiling job (see pages 56–65), begin by applying adhesive to your underlayment, as shown in the top photo. Use the flat end of your trowel to scoop out some adhesive and plop it on your underlayment. Keep the trowel fairly flat to spread the adhesive broadly over the area.

2 SPREAD WITH NOTCHED TROWEL. The next step is to rake the adhesive with the notched edge of your trowel (see page 46 for recommended notch sizes). Whether or not you need to flatten the ridges next will depend on the size of the individual tiles. Smaller tiles mounted to mesh backing often do not require this additional step. Check with the manufacturer of your tile for specifics.

GLASS TILE

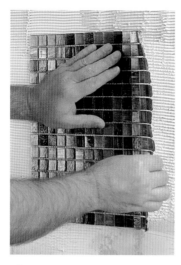

3 POSITION THE SHEETS. With the adhesive in place, begin laying sheets of tile along your reference lines. Press the sheet in place just enough so that it holds its position; you'll set the tiles next.

4 SET THE TILES. The best way to set a sheet of mosaic tiles with a mesh backing is with the shop-made caul described on page 89. Place the caul on a sheet as shown, and tap it with a rubber mallet. Slide the caul across the sheet, tapping as you go to set the tiles.

5 LEVEL THE SHEETS. To level the tiles from sheet to sheet, rotate the caul so it's diagonal, as shown, and tap it with a rubber mallet, working across the sheets.

6 APPLY THE GROUT.
Once all the tile is installed,
allow the adhesive to set
overnight. Then mix up enough
grout to cover a 2- to 4-foot-
square area—remember, the
mosaic tile uses much more
grout than larger tile (see the
chart on page 30 for more on
this). Apply the grout with the
flat portion of the float, and
press it into the joints.

7 SQUEEGEE OFF THE
EXCESS. Now hold your
grout float 45 degrees to the
tile surface and use it as a
squeegee to remove the
excess grout, as shown.

8 REMOVE ANY RESIDUE.
To remove the remaining
grout residue, start with clean,
dry cheesecloth. This will
remove the bulk of the grout
without washing out the grout
lines. Follow this with a just-
damp sponge to wipe off
the last of the grout. Allow
the grout to dry fully, buff off
any haze, and apply a sealer
according to the manufac-
turer's directions.

GLASS TILE

Setting Large Tiles

Larger individual glass tiles are installed much like other field tile, except for how the adhesive is applied.

1 APPLY THE ADHE-SIVE. Once you've attached the appropriate underlayment (see pages 72–75) and have marked any reference lines (see pages 56–65), apply adhesive with the appropriate-sized notched trowel (see page 46).

2 FLATTEN THE ADHE-SIVE. Next you'll want to flatten the ridges of the adhesive so they can't be seen through the tile. Be careful not to redistribute the adhesive—all you're trying to do here is knock off the ridges, leaving a uniform layer of adhesive.

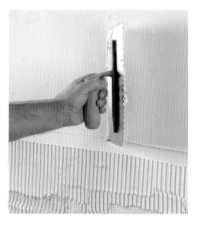

3 CLEAN THE TILES. Just as any flaws in the underlayment and adhesive can be seen through a tile, any dirt or debris on the back of the tile will also be visible. So take the time to clean the backs of your tiles with a clean cloth dipped in acetone before you set them.

4 BACK-BUTTER TILES. Many glass tile manufacturers recommend that you back-butter the tiles (page 85) to make sure you have 100% adhesive coverage. Back-buttering will also help prevent a condition unique to glass tile called "ghosting" that occurs behind the glass due to its translucent nature. Even with proper adhesive coverage, some ghosting is still likely to occur and should be considered normal.

5 SET THE TILES. Now you can set the tile, using the appropriate-sized spacers. Press each tile into the adhesive with a slight twisting motion to better spread the adhesive. Stop occasionally and lift off a tile to check for adhesive coverage. With glass tile you're always looking for 100% coverage. Once all the tile is in place, let

the adhesive dry overnight. Then apply grout as you would for two-step mosaic tiles, as described on page 189.

GLASS TILE

9

Troubleshooting and Repair

IT'S PRETTY OBVIOUS when a tile is cracked or broken, so troubleshooting is fairly straightforward. Tile repair is also simple if you take it one step at a time. Diagnosing grout problems is easy, but repairing grout can be a hassle, depending on the scope of the job. Small jobs are easy; large jobs—like replacing all the grout in a shower—are both time-consuming and messy. In this chapter we'll show you how to troubleshoot and repair common tile and grout problems.

Common Tile Problems

If you find cracked or broken tiles (see below), your first order of business is to determine what caused the problem. You need to know if the failure was caused by external forces (such as dropping a heavy object on the tile) or by internal forces (an improper adhesive bond, moisture, or movement in the materials). If the failure was caused by an external force, you can usually remove and replace the damaged tile(s) as described on pages 197–201.

If you think the problem was caused by internal forces, first remove the damaged tile and inspect the adhesive bond. The adhesive should be distributed evenly between the backer board and the tile. If the bulk of the adhesive is on the tile, the backer board may have been covered with dirt or dust, which prevented a good bond. When the adhesive is mostly on the backer board, it's likely that the adhesive skinned over before the tile was installed—again preventing a good bond. If the tile is installed in a wet area and it's wet under the tile, the grout may have failed; see the opposite page.

CRACKED TILES. A cracked tile that's still solidly attached to the backer board in a dry area needs replacing only if you're annoyed by the crack. In wet areas, cracked tiles should always be replaced.

BROKEN TILES. Whether a broken tile is in a wet or dry area, it should be replaced: The sharp shards of tile can cause a serious injury.

Common Grout Problems

When grout fails, it usually cracks or crumbles (see the photos below). In either case, the failed grout should be removed and replaced; see pages 202–204 for instructions on how to do this. Before you replace grout in a wet area, make sure to inspect to see whether moisture has managed to seep past the grout. If it has, odds are that it will have damaged the adhesive bond between the tile and backer board and the tile may need replacing (see pages 197–201).

CRACKED GROUT JOINTS. The most common cause of cracks in grout joints is lack of expansion joints (see pages 16–17). Flexible expansion joints allow for movement. If hard grout is installed and movement occurs, the grout will crack.

CRUMBLING GROUT JOINTS. Crumbling grout is most often caused by improperly mixed grout. In wet areas it can also result when the grout sealer fails and moisture starts to break down the grout.

Removing Stains on Tile

There are a number of tile cleaners available that do a decent job of removing stains on tile. A homemade, inexpensive solution is to mix 1 cup of vinegar in a gallon of water. This mild acid mix works great—just make sure to rinse off the tile thoroughly after cleaning.

1 **SPRAY ON THE CLEANER.** Many tile cleaners come in handy spray bottles (like the one shown in the photo at left). Just spray directly onto the soiled area and wipe it off. For tougher stains, allow the cleaner to soak for 15 minutes.

2 **SCRUB AND RINSE THE TILE.** For really stubborn stains, you may need to scrub the tile with a stiff-bristle brush (upper right photo) or a nylon pad. Then rinse the area with clean water (bottom photo).

ACID CLEANERS

You'll find a number of acid cleaners wherever you buy tile. These should be used only as a last resort because they're quite dangerous to work with. If you do use an acid cleaner, make sure you have adequate ventilation, and wear eye and skin protection. You'll also want to wear a charcoal-cartridge-type respirator to protect your lungs from fumes.

Replacing Damaged Tile

Replacing a tile can be easy or difficult, depending on what it's made of and how well it's bonded to the underlayment. Softer tiles like ceramic, terra-cotta, and quarry tend to be easier to remove than harder tiles like porcelain and glass.

1 REMOVE THE GROUT. To remove a tile, start by removing the grout surrounding the tile. Depending on the thickness of the grout line, this can be done with a utility knife, a knife for scoring backer board (as shown here), or a grout saw or grout-removal attachment (see page 202).

2 DRILL A FRACTURE HOLE. The next step is to further break up the tile to make it easier to remove. But before you do this, it's a good idea to drill a hole in the center of the tile to create a fracture point. This fracture point helps contain the breaks to the tile and also helps create easily removable chunks. Use a drill

fitted with a masonry or glass and tile bit (page 43) to drill the hole. Make sure to stop as soon as you pass through the tile to prevent damage to the underlayment. If the tile is part of a wet install, skip this step so you don't puncture the waterproofing membrane underneath the tile.

3 TAP TO BREAK UP TILE. Now you can break the tile up into manageable chucks. Wearing eye protection, strike the tile sharply with a hammer, as shown. Try to strike near the fracture hole, as this makes it easier to break up the tile.

4 PRY OUT LARGE CHUNKS. If you can get the claws of a claw hammer under any of the large chucks, do so and pry out the larger pieces. Keep the head of the hammer in the damaged area to prevent damage to the surrounding tiles.

5 **CHISEL OUT SMALLER PIECES.** Switch to a cold chisel to get out the smaller pieces (make sure to wear eye protection). Angle the tip of the chisel at the base of the tile and strike it lightly with a hammer. Be especially careful around the perimeter of the tile to keep from damaging surrounding tiles.

6 **REMOVE THE OLD ADHESIVE.** You may be able to remove some adhesive with a putty knife, as shown. Older, more brittle adhesive will need to be removed with a chisel and hammer. Strike the chisel gently to keep from damaging the underlayment. In wet areas, carefully inspect the underlayment to see whether there is any water damage. If there is, consider applying a trowel-on membrane (see page 34).

7 APPLY NEW ADHESIVE.
After you've removed the tile and its adhesive, use a vacuum to thoroughly remove any dust and debris that could prevent a good bond with the new adhesive. Then mix up some adhesive and apply it to the underlayment with either a putty knife, a trowel, or a notched margin trowel (page 47). Alternatively, you can back-butter the tile as described on page 85 and as shown in the top right photo here.

Q U I C K   F I X

Tile Repair Mortar

Need to install just a tile or two and don't want to buy a 40-pound bag of thin-set? Check the aisle where you buy tile to see whether the store carries small containers of tile repair mortar, like the one shown in the bottom photo. Note that many of these mixes contain portland cement, which is caustic. If your mix does, be sure to wear rubber gloves, a long-sleeved shirt, eye protection, and a respirator to keep dust out of your lungs.

8 INSTALL THE REPLACEMENT TILE.
Press the replacement tile in place so that it compresses the adhesive. Then pull it back out and check the back for adhesive coverage— you're looking for at least 80% coverage; 90% to 95% is preferred. If necessary, add more adhesive and replace the tile. When you achieve proper coverage, leave the tile in place, adding spacers if necessary to set the grout lines and/or lock the tile in place.

9 REMOVE ANY EXCESS THIN-SET. Once the replacement tile is installed, take the time to remove any adhesive that has squeezed out into the grout lines. Depending on the width of your grout lines, this can be done with a dental pick (page 48) or the edge of a putty knife, as shown here. Allow the adhesive to set overnight before grouting, as described on pages 96–98.

Replacing Grout

There are several ways to remove old grout. The width of the grout lines should dictate the one you choose. Grout lines wider than ⅛" can be tackled with a grout saw (see below) or a rotary tool (see page 50). Grout lines narrower than ⅛"—common on ceramic tiles with built-in spacers—are best removed with a grout-removal attachment (see below). Whichever method you choose, you need to know that this is a messy job—you'll be producing a lot of dust. So use drop cloths to seal the area you're working in, and wear eye protection as well as a respirator to keep the fine grout dust out of your lungs.

USING A GROUT SAW. A grout saw does an admirable job of removing grout—it just takes a lot of elbow grease to get the job done. These saws are great for small repairs but are unsuitable for large jobs. For large jobs, consider using a rotary tool.

USING A GROUT-REMOVAL ATTACH-MENT. The grout-removal attachment shown here is manufactured by Dremel (www.dremel.com) for their rotary tool. Tabs on the plastic shroud that fits over the end of the tool ride in the space between the tiles. This automatically tracks the tool, so its grinding tip slips into the gap between the tiles to quickly remove grout. This surprisingly simple design works great and will finish a large job in no time at all.

1 CHECK FOR LOOSE
TILES. Once you've removed
the grout, it's a good idea to go
from tile to tile, checking for
loose tiles. If you're removing
grout in a wet area because it
failed, this check will show
whether moisture seeped under
any tiles and caused the adhesive to fail. The handle of a putty
knife makes a good striker. Just
lightly tap each tile in its center,
as shown. A hollow sound indi-
cates a failed bond and that the
tile should be replaced (pages
197–201) before re-grouting.

2 SCRAPE OFF GROUT
AROUND TILE EDGES.
Now carefully inspect the tiles.
You'll probably still find some
grout stuck to the rounded edges
on some of the tiles. This can be
quickly scraped off with the edge
of a putty knife, as shown in the
middle photo.

3 REMOVE OLD GROUT
DUST. With all the grout
removed, let the dust settle and
then go back over your entire tile
area with a vacuum to remove
the sanding dust. Allow the dust
to settle one more time and
vacuum again. This may seem
extreme, but any dust left in the
grout lines can prevent the fresh
grout from bonding properly to
the tile.

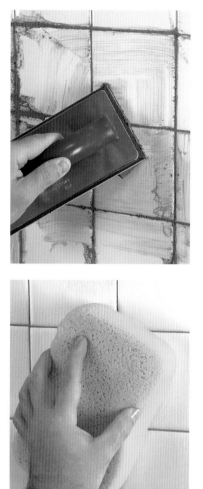

4 APPLY FRESH GROUT. Mix up a batch of grout sufficient to grout a 2- to 4-foot-square area. Allow it to slake (page 96), and apply it to the tile with a grout float. Press the grout into the gaps between the tiles and then angle the float at 45 degrees to the tile. Use the float as a squeegee to scrape off the excess grout.

5 SPONGE OFF THE EXCESS. With the excess removed, switch to a damp sponge to wipe away any residue. Rinse the sponge frequently and change the water in your bucket often. Allow the grout to dry, and buff off the haze with a clean, soft cloth. When the grout has dried a minimum of two days, apply a sealer (see page 98). To toughen up grout in wet areas, consider damp-curing the grout, as described on page 97.

Cleaning Grout

One of the best ways you can both maintain grout and keep it looking good is to periodically clean it with a grout cleaner/sealer, as described in the sidebar below.

1 SPRAY ON CLEANER. To clean grout, spray on the cleaner and allow it to soak in the recommended time. Some cleaners suggest a second application before wiping or scrubbing the grout line.

2 SCRUB WITH A TOOTHBRUSH. Tough grout stains often require a little elbow grease to remove the stain. An ordinary toothbrush does a great job of concentrating the scrubbing power on the narrow grout lines. Periodically rinse the toothbrush with clean water as you continue to work on stains.

P R O   T I P

Grout Cleaners

You'll find standard grout cleaners wherever tile is sold. Some versions (like the one shown here) also seal the grout, as well. If you notice that your grout gets dirty quickly, consider using a professional-strength sealer once you've cleaned the tiles. Pros often use a special type of sealer called an "impregnator," commonly used in commercial facilities. You'll generally find these only at a tile-supply house for pros.

TROUBLESHOOTING AND REPAIR

Index

Metric Equivalency Chart

Inches to millimeters and centimeters

INCHES	MM	CM	INCHES	CM	INCHES	CM
1/8	3	0.3	9	22.9	30	76.2
1/4	6	0.6	10	25.4	31	78.7
3/8	10	1.0	11	27.9	32	81.3
1/2	13	1.3	12	30.5	33	83.8
5/8	16	1.6	13	33.0	34	86.4
3/4	19	1.9	14	35.6	35	88.9
7/8	22	2.2	15	38.1	36	91.4
1	25	2.5	16	40.6	37	94.0
1 1/4	32	3.2	17	43.2	38	96.5
1 1/2	38	3.8	18	45.7	39	99.1
1 3/4	44	4.4	19	48.3	40	101.6
2	51	5.1	20	50.8	41	104.1
2 1/2	64	6.4	21	53.3	42	106.7
3	76	7.6	22	55.9	43	109.2
3 1/2	89	8.9	23	58.4	44	111.8
4	102	10.2	24	61.0	45	114.3
4 1/2	114	11.4	25	63.5	46	116.8
5	127	12.7	26	66.0	47	119.4
6	152	15.2	27	68.6	48	121.9
7	178	17.8	28	71.1	49	124.5
8	203	20.3	29	73.7	50	127.0

mm = millimeters   cm = centimeters

PHOTO CREDITS

Crossville
(www.crossvilleinc.com):
page 13 (top photo),
page 14.

Hakatai
(www.hakatai.com):
page 13 (bottom photo),
page 15.

Bostik
(www.bostik.com):
page 29 (both photos),
page 180 (bottom photo),
page 181 (bottom photo).